Philipp Staab
Adaptation

X-Texts on Culture and Society

X-TEXTS

The supposed 'end of history' turned out to be the end of certainty. Today we are dealing with the urgent questions posed by generations X, Y and Z. If we are to navigate a world in turmoil, we need insightful, reality-based guidance. That is what our **X-TEXTS** series sets out to provide: incisive analyses of society in our time, a forum for understanding and dissecting the trends, separating the wheat from the chaff. We believe that the issues at stake demand public debate beyond the ivory towers, and are pleased to be making these important contributions accessible to a wider audience.

Philipp Staab is professor of sociology of work, political economy and technological change at Humboldt-Universität zu Berlin and co-director of the Einstein Center Digital Future. In his research, he combines topics of work, social structure analysis, sociology of technology and political economy, working on the transformations of digital capitalism, ecological conflicts in late-modern societies, their changes in the context of war and the political crises that arise from all these contexts.

Philipp Staab

Adaptation

Freedom, Hope and Politics after Modernity

Translated from the German by Meredith Dale

[transcript]

Bibliographic information published by the Deutsche Nationalbibliothek
The Deutsche Nationalbibliothek lists this publication in the Deutsche Nationalbibliografie; detailed bibliographic data are available online at https://dnb.dnb.de

Originally published in German as "Anpassung: Leitmotiv der nächsten Gesellschaft" (Suhrkamp, 2022)

2026 © Philipp Staab

transcript Verlag | Hermannstraße 26 | D-33602 Bielefeld | live@transcript-verlag.de

Cover design: Kordula Röckenhaus
Translation: Meredith Dale
Copy-editing: Louise Pain
https://doi.org/10.14361/9783839457511
Print-ISBN: 978-3-8376-8046-1 | PDF-ISBN: 978-3-8394-5751-1
ISSN of series: 2364-6616 | eISSN of series: 2747-3775

Contents

1. Introduction: Metamorphoses of adaptation

> Behind all the objectifications,
> sooner or later the question of
> *acceptance* arises and with it anew
> the old question: *how do we wish to*
> *live?*
> Ulrich Beck, 1986[1]

> Och, if I were going there, I
> wouldn't start from here...

Might it be the case that the modern ideals of progress, emancipation and democratisation are simply the wrong starting point for an analysis of the present state of society and its foreseeable future? That an analysis that reifies modernisation may fail to register real changes occurring in society? That we need to define both the present and the prospective society in defensive – rather than expansive – terms? Might it be the case that society's true lodestar is not individualisation but adaptation, not progress but survival?

Two decades into the twenty-first century, that certainly seems plausible. The global financial crisis of 2008 took the system to the brink of collapse, only for enormous resources to be poured into 'rescuing' pillars regarded as 'too big to fail'. Rather than striking out on a transformative path, the shards were gathered up and stuck back together. Rather than a conscious fresh start, the response was the same old practices of *structural adjustment* to the requirements of capitalism that have always characterised the policies of the International Monetary Fund and World Bank. After another decade of crisis, societies across the world are still seeking real alternatives. But wave after wave of disruption – including the

Covid-19 pandemic – has locked them into reactive mode, from the heights of politics and economics to the nitty-gritty of everyday life and personal affairs. Russia's invasion of Ukraine has forced Western societies into a defensive stance, from which they will not be able to escape by ramping up arms spending. Their version of internationalism is not global progress and solidarity in the style of the classical left of the twentieth century, but fortifying defences as and when dangers appear on their radar. And looming behind these acute crises, of course, is the ultimate threat of climate catastrophe.

It is arguably very difficult to tackle the risks proactively. Modern human society apparently has a destructive relationship to the natural world (while massively overestimating its own ability to control events). Even those who still believe it might be possible to influence the trajectory of capitalism – calling for another 'great transformation'[2] to blunt its destructive logic through social re-embedding[3] – are generally less sanguine about the chances of actually realising such a shift. This is especially clear in relation to climate change,[4] where the frame has narrowed to merely *adaptive responses*: mitigation and resilience to survive the inevitable.

Yet contemporary social analysis remains dominated by the modernisation paradigm, in particular the ideal of individualism (self-realisation). The original modernisation liberated the individual from the repressive ties of blood, soil and church, shattering the 'mechanical solidarity'[5] of pre-modern communities, exploding feudal power relations, and substituting in their place free association of individuals, dynamisation of the social order, and democratisation of personal 'life chances'.[6]

Most accounts would see this logic continuing into late modernity, with a further radicalisation of the freedom to individuate, to singularise the self.[7] Modernisation still means liberation in the sense of expanding opportunities for the individual.[8]

Or at least the possibility thereof. The formats of power associated with (late) modernity have in fact been thoroughly ambivalent, piling ever more responsibility onto the individual, demanding that we choose and curate our lifestyles. Contemporary capitalism forces us to be the architects of our own fortune – with no one but ourselves to blame for failure. Like it or not, we must operate within a dynamic order, pursuing our life chances amidst an illusion of meritocracy.[9]

Emancipation and authenticity tend to be idealised, while adaptation is frowned upon as a characteristic of traditional societies that shun personal development and demand conformity. Yet escaping such contexts – village, church, family or rigid gender roles – generates its own adaptation pressures: once the traditional ties have been broken, *there is no alternative* to individual responsibility. Adaptation is unavoidable. If you want to 'get on', you must obey rules over which you have no meaningful influence. The transactions are non-negotiable. The price of a house, a car and a fitted kitchen in the post-war era was conformity to a standardised way of life. In order to secure their swanky apartment, electric SUV and Instagrammable holidays, today's professional must bow to the demands of flexibilisation, exhibit complete self-motivation and even fund their own pension. In other words, adaptation *forces*, adaptation is repression.

The idea that adaptation is the opposite of freedom builds on a string of assumptions that appear increasingly implausible today. As a guiding principle, self-realisation is highly contingent. The opportunities of individualism only open up to the broader population once the fundamental issues of *survival* have been resolved. The fulfilment of basic needs like food, shelter and a modicum of social security is, as Ronald Inglehart demonstrates, a necessary condition for the cultural primacy of self-actualisation.[10] From a materialist perspective, that is precisely why the ideal of self-realisation (or individualism) is so closely bound up with the modernisation of society. By driving economic growth and relativising the question of naked survival, modernisation creates the essential preconditions for the flourishing of individual subjectivity.

The decisive point here is that the implicit consensus that our material existence is secure no longer holds. Thus, the systematic return of questions of survival – which is itself an effect of the modern self-realisation paradigm – must form the linchpin of any investigation of the present, and particularly the forthcoming society.

In and of itself, that insight is nothing new. Back in the mid-1980s Ulrich Beck was already discussing the problems generated by modernisation in terms of individualisation and risk.[11] Beck argues that the negative side effects of modernisation become lodged in the public consciousness, creating ever-increasing demand for new forms of risk compensation. The unfortunate outcomes of mankind's supposed domination of nature – environmental degradation, chemical spills and the latent threat of nuclear war – formed the backdrop to this reappearance of fundamental existential questions.[12] Beck shows how the modern self-realisation paradigm brings forth its own crises of self-preservation. The adaptive response to these is both an effect and a precondition of the possibilities of individualisation. If we take this observation seriously, we can no longer simply denounce adaptation as the opposite of freedom. Instead, adaptation turns out to be its precondition – and a fundamental paradigm of a society confronted with systemic (modernisation-related) threats to its own survival.

This is especially pertinent given that risks, as Beck indicates, tend to be managed rather than resolved, while ongoing modernisation generates new and cascading risks. Existential threats are potentiated, further heightening the sense of a loss of control. This is most obvious in the climate debate, where we can now enumerate the repercussions in great detail: loss of biodiversity (species extinction), specific health risks, rising sea levels, and dramatic shifts when particular *tipping points* are crossed. In other words, we are dealing with a proliferation of secondary dangers.

However well the risks are managed, pressure of adaptation will remain. Even where effective action would theoretically still be possible, the capacity to do so remains conspicuously limited. In the political mainstream, 'manageable climate change' still means a world whose average temperatures are 1.5 to 2° C higher than they were in the pre-industrial age – while the current warming of roughly 1° C is already wreaking havoc, from extinction and disease to devastating forest fires and climate-driven depopulation of entire regions. The question is not *whether* threats to survival will arise but *how grave* they will be and *whom* they will affect.

Comparable problems are glaringly obvious in the economic and geopolitical spheres. Global capitalism is chronically crisis-prone, requiring permanent state intervention to save it from collapse. Its economic practices have brought the ecosphere to the brink of doom, while enriching a tiny elite at the expense of the masses. At the same time, over-exploitation of the natural environment has itself become a crucial source of economic instability, while alternative political economies are nowhere to be seen. The swansong of US hegemony puts questions of geopolitical self-preservation back on the table. Europe's Cold War fears of nuclear annihilation have given way to anxiety over waning US interest. It is increasingly obvious that we are generating incalculable dangers that we can perhaps temporarily 'externalise',[13] but certainly do not have 'under control'.

So, almost forty years on from Beck's *Risk Society*, the associated hopes have been largely disappointed. In the 1980s and 1990s it was still possible to believe that Beck's brand of individualism would enable us to contain the risks: that consumer boycotts, recycling, lifestyle choices and political pressure could rein in the excesses of risk capitalism, that peace activism could bring belligerents to their senses. Those hopes of a better, or what Beck calls a 'reflexive modernisation' now appear absurdly overoptimistic.[14] Neither subpolitical risk containment, which has certainly occurred to an extent, nor reflexive management of the consequences of modernisation have been able to avert escalating existential threats. Instead, the reflexive paradigm of converting unpredictable dangers into calculable risks has apparently exhausted its possibilities. Nuclear power stations (and increasingly also weather events) are uninsurable because the magnitude of potential claims would plunge even the largest insurer into bankruptcy. The likelihood of devastating forest fires and the pace of rising sea levels may be calculable, but their predictability is scant consolation. Individualisation gains have systematically exacerbated survival risks, generating increasingly tangible pressure of adaptation.

But how should one describe a society that is characterised more by the problems of survival than the benefits of self-realisation? Whose guiding lights are not progress, emancipation or individual liberty, but adjustment and adaptation? Intellectual interventions building on the perspective of adaptation have already begun sketching the outlines of societies moving beyond ruthless prioritisation of the self. In place of the classical metaphors of body and machine, the emblem of today's social analysis is the fungus. What the modern reflex perceived as a nuisance to be eliminated or a resource to be harvested, consumed or sold at market has now become the symbol of a paradigmatic after-modern way of life.

Eva von Redecker proposes fungi as a counter-model to the isolating individualism of the modern age. Many fungi form extensive underground root-like structures (mycelia) that supply nutrients to trees, receiving in return sugars generated by photosynthesis.[15] Von Redecker conceptualises this as a way of life based on symbiosis, reciprocity and solidarity, upon which we could draw in our relationships with one another and with our natural environment. We need only decide to do so, she asserts.

While von Redecker's romantic take still revolves around the heroic, emancipation-seeking and thus fundamentally modern subject, other fungi-related theories go a good deal further. In her economic and social analysis of the matsutake mushroom, US-based anthropologist Anna Lowenhaupt Tsing describes a fundamentally adaptive society that has abandoned any hope of modern progress.[16] Like the risks of late modernity themselves, matsutake are an unintentional side effect of modernisation, as they grow only in industrially managed forests. After Japan shifted to more natural forestry methods towards the end of the twentieth century (and the fallout from Chernobyl made fungi from European forests unsafe to eat), a new centre of matsutake-gathering emerged on the West Coast of the United States. Tsing observes a specific arboreal ecology, and with it a specific social ecology, emerging around the matsutake mushroom in forests ruined by capitalist exploitation. Matsutake sustain the wounded forest without healing it. They are aides of adaptation in multiple respects. Quite aside from the woodland ecology, they also form the basis of niche economies for the precarised groups that gather them in the forests of Oregon. Here, Tsing found outsiders and outlaws, and above all Asian immigrants whose sense of community remains foreign to the realities of life in modern America. Together, they form a community of adaptive precarity encompassing trees, fungi and humans, which Tsing interprets as reflecting the condition of a globally networked but fragmented world.

What we are starting to see here is a different, non-modern conception of adaptation. This is no heroic choice of symbiosis, no vision of a society to come. Instead, the social ecology of society itself is imagined as an effect of capitalist destruction and comprehensive loss, while adaptation is a condition of the capacity to make a life in a world where there can be no return to progress and modernity. Tsing sets out to explore the possibilities of 'life in capitalist ruins',[17] where the relationship between power and personal meaning is thrown into sharp relief. Here we begin to discern the contours of a subjectivity after modernity, where visible and invisible networks of solidarity make it possible not only to survive biologically but to thrive socially. Tsing finds the corresponding sense of meaning in the interactions of survival, in niches occupied by unlikely alliances of precarised human and non-human life forms. These provide a glimpse of a possible future, in which accidental ecologies and non-modern communities create the possibility of a 'successful life'.

Our vantage point for this tentative preview of the next society lies on the margins of the present one, where the promises of modernity were abandoned long ago: a ruined forest where uprooted humans are largely left to fend for themselves, where the ambulance never comes on time.[18] One could argue that it is not just modernity, but society itself that has been abandoned here. The social division of labour, as the driving force of capitalist integration, naturally still forms the backdrop; ultimately, the fungi are destined for the world market. But the positive aspects – solidarity, freedom, meaning – are properties of the micro-communities of the dispossessed. In a very fundamental sense they are fending for themselves at the margins of society. What we are looking at here are adaptive communities, not an adaptive society.

We encounter the latter where society is mobilised in response to an acute threat, as was the case with Covid-19. The pandemic has often been discussed as a preview of the kind of crisis that will characterise the twenty-first century. The pandemic was not just an outcome of our society's brutal exploitation of the natural environment. It also presaged the present and future climate crisis, in the sense that it posed acute danger to human life, mercilessly exposed deficits of political management, and elicited fundamental – if temporary – reconfigurations of the political economy. It was also a crisis of capitalism, not only because the underlying relationship to nature can be characterised as genuinely capitalist,[19] but also because the associated economic and social repercussions delivered significant shocks to the capitalist mode of economy itself. The fundamental shifts revealed by this paradigmatic crisis of adaptation tell us a great deal about the character of the adaptive society. The pandemic suddenly transformed the neglected problems of a vulnerable and self-destructive society – the questions of reproduction and survival – into the core concerns of everyday life, and placed them at the very centre of public debate. For a moment, fantasies of individual liberty and self-realisation took a back seat as strategies for protecting life moved to the fore, along with an emphasis on social interdependencies and interconnectedness. That dynamic led to profound changes in modes of societal coordination: the impromptu division of the labour force into essential and implicitly non-essential workers springs to mind immediately, as do the temporary mobilisations of volunteers and military personnel. For a time survival took precedence, sidelining activities that normally enjoy much greater social status and prestige. For a brief period, in a social praxis of adaptation, the spotlight fell on the tasks and professions that are most central to the preservation of society. This time, the ambulance did arrive on time. Collective adaptation, it transpires, is a specific form of labour directed towards maintaining life and conducted within the foundational sectors of the economy.[20] Adaptation, it would appear, is to a significant extent a matter of infrastructure. It prioritises the general over the specific, collective duty and individual responsibility over competitive self-realisation.

So what else do we find, if we place adaptation at the heart of social analysis? What concepts of emancipation, what ideas about time and history, what promises of a subjectively good life, and what political perspectives characterise an adaptive society? As these genuinely sociological questions reveal, there is much more at stake than mere biological survival. The problems of self-preservation that characterise our discussions about society need to be considered as questions concerning the ways people make sense of their lives. For the way we live forms the elementary basis of all complex societal structures, and is in turn sustained and reproduced by them. If we are to grasp adaptation as social praxis, then we are dealing first and foremost with the configurations of an adaptive way of living. The central point of reference here is Max Weber's famous analysis of the social origins of capitalist modernisation. As Weber argues, these lie in specific horizons of meaning that are predicated on the possibility of future salvation.[21] In his treatise on the Protestant ethic, Weber lays out how the Protestant frame of eternity fostered the this-worldly asceticism that spurred capitalist development.

It is not hard to see how such a perspective also raises questions concerning power and authority in society. The way life is conducted structures the social, from the configurations of inequality to the modes of political power. It makes a difference whether one views liberal democracy from the perspective of a labourer or a manager. The former sees and despises an exploitative system; the latter affirms the source of her success and recognition. Any critique of society must thus start from the ways of life that shape it.

The decisive point for any contemporary social analysis is that the *possibility* of 'a way of life' can no longer be assumed where the threats to society become existential. Instead, a basal realisation that the modern way of life is fundamentally endangered by its own unintended side effects is inherent to the adaptive society. The adaptive constellation thus raises the sociologically decisive question: What ways of social life are possible where survival is endangered?

The short answer to this question, which I will unravel piece by piece in the following chapters, is that, firstly, an adaptive society generates its own sources of meaning through an adaptive praxis whose basic outlines are rejection of the modern concept of personal emancipation, reflexive renunciation of the ideal of progress, and a post-narcissistic ideal of life based on competence and responsibility. Secondly, life in the adaptive society generates a specific political dynamic that I would define as a *technocratic yearning*. In so doing, I treat adaptation as a genuinely *social* phenomenon. My interest is to conduct a neutral examination of adaptation as a central social praxis, not to praise or bury it. We need to dispense with the normative connotations acquired in the course of the modern age. In that tradition, 'adaptation' and 'adjustment' often have a cynical or denunciatory tinge: cynical, where adaptation means stabilising a social order that actually needs to be changed; denunciatory where adaptation is understood as an affront to the individual's right to self-realisation. I therefore start – in Chapter 2 – by discussing the traditional sociological understanding of adaptation and siting it in relation to the current crisis of late modernity. It transpires that all the relevant examples of societal adaptation arise, as intimated above, in contexts of a normative primacy of self-realisation. Switching the perspective to existential problems opens the door to a new understanding of adaptation as an integrated praxis of individual and collective transformation and a precondition for liberty in the adaptive society. At the same time this challenges the modern norm of personal emancipation. Adapting our understanding of adaptation also bears – for all the inherent contradictions – its own perspective on freedom. If the cultural primacy of individualism is transcended, its burdens can also fade away.[22]

On the other hand, the adaptive society represents a categorical departure from the classic modern understanding of progress as constant optimisation and boundless self-realisation. The rise of the adaptation paradigm, as manifested in concepts like mitigation and resilience, is therefore associated with a collapse of temporal horizons, as I explain in Chapter 3. The adaptive society, it follows, is already further advanced than most of the social science observing it. Its praxis, its way of life, has abandoned the project of social progress, of heroically 'conquering the future' through relentless betterment and limitless individualism. Here again an inherent perspective of liberation shimmers through. Renouncing progress also relieves the subject of responsibility for the discredited project of social optimisation.

Relief from the burdens of self-realisation and from responsibility for a destructive modern project is, of course, a perspective of negative freedom. It will be liberating if we no longer have to make a show of our individuality; if we no longer have to emphasise the solitary over the collective; and if we no longer have to pretend that we will be able to solve planetary problems just by putting in a little more effort. Seeking positive perspectives on freedom, I turn in Chapter 4 to a body of literature that provides an affirmative concept of adaptation as a praxis free of the compulsion to aggrandise and accelerate,[23] a creative and rebellious praxis challenging cultural norms and social rules. The focus on survival lends the adaptive revolt – as manifested, for example, in the new climate movement – a political logic of its own, expressed as a desire for rational technocracy.

This technocratic yearning reappears in Chapter 5, in which I turn to the adaptive society in action. I tackle this question empirically, using qualitative interviews with essential workers during the Covid-19 pandemic. My intention here is to focus attention on the key actors of adaptation, the workers most centrally involved in the collective adjustment of society. One could call them the adaptive avant-garde. I understand their experiences during the acute phase of crisis as a natural experiment in adaptive praxis and its interpretation. The interviews reveal their criticisms concerning their own situation and society at large, and their perspectives on freedom. The subjects describe massive overwork and stress within a social order they perceive to be fundamentally bifurcated – a division they attribute to narcissistic cultural influences and a systemic crisis of political capacity. As the interviews reveal, they ultimately hope for relief through a depoliticisation of survival risks, implemented by a competent technocracy.

The concluding chapter explores the implicit political vectors associated with the adaptive society. The central political interest associated with survival is neither democratisation nor personal emancipation. Instead, we see a longing to address existential threats without political strife; this is true of protesters and technocrats alike, and of political theories that take as their starting point questions of survival. Under the primacy of survival, depoliticising risk becomes the decisive condition of political legitimacy. In sharp contrast to the age of individualism, prioritising survival points us towards a civilisation where freedom is defined in terms of depoliticisation. *Protective technocracy* is the logical social contract of the adaptive society.

2. The party and the hangover: From surplus to survival

> But it's our only way out: finding,
> together, a territory we can live in.
> This is the new universality.
> *Bruno Latour (2017)*[1]

If human society is going to prioritise survival, adaptation will be absolutely central. But that does not necessarily mean rejecting individualisation. The point is to explore the central mechanisms of adaptation through a shift in perspective from the modernist programme of emancipation to an as yet undefined programme of adaptation. Although adaptation is neither new nor inherently modern, the pressure to adapt in modern society follows a specific logic that we need to understand – and to distinguish from the kind of adaptation that will be required for survival.

In fact, of course, societies are always dealing with problems of adaptation. We must adapt our practices to events and conditions that are beyond our control. So adaptation is change. But not freely chosen. Ever-changing circumstances force us to adapt our everyday lives. This has been true throughout human history. In 'primitive' societies environmental change was the central driver of adaptation. The whims of nature defined what people could hunt and gather, plant and harvest. Any change in the environment automatically compelled them to adapt.

We can identify three principal characteristics of these *original* constellations of adaptation. Firstly, the relevant problems and threats were external to the society; they lay beyond the control of the affected community (or were at least perceived to) and were not negotiable. Secondly, in this context, adaptation was above all a matter of survival: adapt or die. Thirdly, individual and collective adaptation were inseparable. The community survived together. Or not. Adjusting a collective way of life demanded more than merely individuals changing their ways.

Modern societies exhibit similar traits: change is in their DNA, as formations whose stability is inherently dynamic.[2] Living under dynamic stability – predicated on incessant economic growth, technological acceleration, cultural innovation[3] – means accepting permanent change and constantly changing rules. Here, again, adaptation is the normal state of affairs. In fact, it is a precondition of the accelerated modern society: rapid road transport depends on broad acceptance of the highway code; a successful career means obeying the school rules and conforming to the structures and strictures of the labour market. If we want to use new technologies, we have to follow the manual.

At an even more fundamental level, we are learning creatures. We observe and emulate others; we understand other people's expectations and try to live up to them. In this sense, adaptation is an absolute precondition for the existence of society. As the dictionary tells us, adaptation is 'the process of changing to suit different conditions'.[4] Whether it is characteristics, beliefs, customs or forms of behaviour that are subject to change, adaptation is plainly an indispensable precondition for 'participating in social relations and systems based on a division of labour – in other words, for handling the demands of social cooperation and the environment, and thus ultimately for the very existence of human society'.[5]

This makes adaptation an essential element in certain strands of modern sociology, because it solves fundamental societal problems – or really, one could say, *the* central problem of society: what is required to make society possible? There is certainly no reason to assume that people will automatically live together harmoniously, form societies based on trust, and develop a sophisticated division of labour. Quite the opposite. That is the central enigma, which brings us to Talcott Parsons and the Hobbesian problem of order:[6] the emergence of human society was not inevitable, and it demands explanation. Without society, the individual's personal safety can never be secure. As Thomas Hobbes famously wrote, even 'the weakest has strength enough to kill the strongest, either by secret machination, or by confederacy with others, that are in the same danger as himselfe'.[7] Individuals can obviously achieve much more if they work together. But how can cooperation succeed under conditions of such insecurity? This is of course where Hobbes's social contract comes in: the people grant the state a monopoly on the legitimate use of physical force. It is adaptation to that set of rules that enables citizens to live without fear of one another.

Various sociologists before and after Parsons have conceptualised solutions to the Hobbesian problem of order. Émile Durkheim stands out as a theorist of order – and of the consequences of its erosion. It was Durkheim who identified the central role of functional differentiation (the division of labour) in the reproduction of the social order in modern societies.[8] By recognising the role their own work plays in the greater whole, individuals come to understand that they are an essential part of the entity that secures their social existence. In effect, this creates an 'organic' form of solidarity because it is clear – to stick with Durkheim's image – that no single part of the social body can survive without the others. It is the shared norms generated by functional differentiation of labour[9] that form the basis for social cooperation and the integration of the individual.

This is only possible if people obey the rules and heed the norms. In the early version of Parsons's famous AGIL paradigm, *adaptation* subsumes all the activities required to maintain an action system.[10] Appropriate adaptive behaviour is guided by the values that are (re)produced by the cultural system: individuals within a cultural system share a broad consensus about the behavioural adaptations required to maintain their social order. Or as Parsons puts it, 'Order in this sense means that process takes place in conformity.'[11]

Failure to adapt places the individual at risk. And in times of societal crisis, individual experiences may snowball into collective problems. When normality is lost, the social order itself is destabilised. It is no long clear which rules still apply, nor who is still following them at all. Society threatens to descend into anarchy, and its members lose their orientation. Durkheim speaks of 'anomie' and rising rates of suicide.[12] In this school of sociology personal adaptation is simply a condition of a successful life, while a lack of normative ties represents an existential risk.

There is no successful life without adaptation, which remains a precondition for any possibility of self-realisation. Individual prestige, reputation and recognition are all nourished by society itself, presupposing that we act broadly in accordance with the expectations of others. In order to earn respect, one must play by the implicit rules of the institution – be it a graffiti crew, union branch or board of directors. Whether the context is a gang or a university, you need to stay in line if you want to get on.

Let us now move on to consider the sociologists of freedom, who ultimately seek to overcome established power relations. Their interest revolves around the question of what obstructs the expansion of freedom in modern life and what freedoms have been lost in the modernisation process. Their theories of power and freedom are characterised by their (more or less explicit) focus on the individual and personal emancipation. They regard the social order as a system of power that unnecessarily restricts the freedom of the individual. The inherent normativity of these theories prioritises opportunities for self-realisation over functional integration. As far as these authors are concerned, adaptation is not merely the precondition for society, but also one of its problems.

The classical sociologies of freedom thus tend to treat adaptation as a practice for losers, who are to be pitied. The unfolding modernisation process turns everything on its head: industrialisation transforms communities and modes of production; the development of the modern state transforms political organisation; new patterns of spatial and social mobility transform ways of life. Modernisation is a rationalisation process that touches on all spheres of society. As individuals, we experience it as an external force, a new environment that threatens to mutate into an 'iron cage'.[13] Change is driven by a minority. The majority simply have to bend and fit in, for better or worse.

The sociologies of freedom are not interested in the promises of existing structures, the tacit normative consensus. While the theories of order foreground the benefits – efficient modern administration, affordable consumer goods, security and stability –

the sociologists of freedom seek to transcend the bounds of the existing, or at least to find a specific form of freedom under the given conditions. Rather than celebrating the stabilising consensus of bourgeois culture, Max Weber, for example, puts his finger on the problem of obedience and the constraints placed on the individual by burgeoning rational administration. Modernity sweeps away traditional forms of legitimisation, replacing them with dry legal systems. Today we just read the rules, rather than following charismatic leaders or mysterious rituals. The possibilities to resist, the spaces for personal freedom, remain limited. Nevertheless, Weber still regards freedom as the ultimate objective.[14] In this scheme of thinking, a person is free if they dedicate themselves absolutely to the pursuit of a personal value. For example, avoiding eating meat out of personal conviction and consideration for the well-being of other living creatures and disregarding one's own cravings. As such, the question of freedom is absolutely bound up with the focus on power. As well as being the absolute opposite of power, freedom is understood as a way of life (indeed *the* way of life).

Marx is a different kettle of fish, of course, although he also understands adaptation as a necessary individual response to power and circumstance. Work or die. Exploitation or starvation. Those were the stark alternatives faced by the masses during the early industrial era. Freedom lies elsewhere, in a coming world where the tables are turned, where the necessity to adapt is minimised and personal freedom maximised:

> [I]n communist society, where nobody has one exclusive sphere of activity but each can become accomplished in any branch he wishes, society regulates the general production and thus makes it possible for me to do one thing today and another tomorrow, to hunt in the morning, fish in the afternoon, rear cattle in the evening, criticise after dinner, just as I have a mind, without ever becoming hunter, fisherman, herdsman or critic.[15]

To this day, Marx inspires theories that assume falling demand for labour, whether through automation or a structural weakness of capitalism.[16] Instead of mourning the loss of employment and income (and in some cases also of meaningful activity), they see the reduction of socially necessary labour as an opportunity to chisel greater freedom out of the realm of necessity and to expand the possibilities for personal freedom.[17]

Marxian theories tend to take a negative slant on adaptation, identifying it with voluntary or enforced conformism and thus the opposite of emancipation. Herbert Marcuse speaks of 'voluntary compliance',[18] where sociologies of order would merely recognise a successful stabilisation of society. Those critical traditions would still have us trying to unmask (late) modernity's fictions of freedom. As the Frankfurt School's critique of the capitalist culture industry points out,[19] a person may seek to style themselves as unique – for example, by means of tattoos or jewellery – but this will always involve reference to (societal) ideas, fashions and identities. Or if they wish to stand out through their consumer choices, they will generally be choosing among products whose variance remains so limited (despite innovations like modularisation) that it is actually rather strange that they can be used to shape individual identities at all. A car is just a car, even if the buyer can choose any combination of ten different colours, ten types of engine and six kinds of wheels. These goods represent a hollow promise of freedom, for which the bearers of the 'happy consciousness'[20] sacrifice months of their lives to the 'pleasures' of capitalist exploitation: physical exhaustion, mental alienation, pressure to perform and conform. In the end, the dominant modes of individualisation are actually just expressions of repressive adaptation.

From this perspective, we can blame warped understandings of freedom on the temptations of the culture industry. Conformism is a structural compulsion. What alternative do people have, if capitalism is the only option? If welfare entitlements demand complex means testing?[21] If politicians treat citizens as consumers of democracy?[22] And if the most powerful technological innovations of the past fifty years are employed largely to push advertising and online shopping as the key to self-realisation?[23] Emancipatory critiques finger the tension between a conformity-enforcing welfare state (need must be proven according to a set of predefined criteria, benefits are distributed under pain of legitimation[24]) and the right to existential security (as a precondition for realising individual opportunities). They criticise a technocratic polity that reduces its citizens to mere onlookers,[25] protest against the manipulative effects of surveillance technologies,[26] and condemn privatisation of the public sphere into the hands of powerful corporations.[27] According to such analyses, the institutionalised compulsion to adapt functions as a vehicle of oppression, thwarting any chance of emancipation. Any critical sociology that explicitly or implicitly foregrounds a subject-centred concept of emancipation must automatically be sceptical of the idea of adaptation. In this line of thought, adaptation is a question of power in society.

This strand of modern sociology seeks to understand and explain the causes of pressure to adapt. Unlike 'primitive' societies, to whom the demands of the natural world appeared external, the forces of compulsion in modern societies are evidently man-made. What robs workers of their freedom is an economic system controlled by bourgeois property owners and defended by powerful political actors. Power lies in the hands of bureaucrats and managers, with little or no democratic legitimation. Executives at Google and Facebook decide what we see. The possibility of attribution places adaptation in the realm of the negotiable, as the object of ire and above all of demands. A democratisation of opportunities for self-realisation is conceivable. As conflicts over 'life chances',[28] they form a central theme of modernity.

Three elements characterise the established understanding of adaptation. Firstly, it is acknowledged that the threats are man-made and inherent to society. Secondly, individual emancipation is the battleground, while conflicts concerning survival take a back seat. And thirdly, society is imagined as a central source of pressure to adapt. This has generated a critique driven by the idea of individual emancipation, whose core demand is the democratisation of self-realisation. Personal adaptation is seen as a repressive imposition, while the possibility of collective pressure to adapt is not even entertained, because the liberal social contract supposedly resolves all questions of survival. Putting collective problems of survival back on the table throws up questions over the imagined 'natural state' and systematically challenges the modern social contract as the source of political legitimacy.

From individualism to collective survival

The cultural primacy of individualism has seen opportunities for citizens of the open industrialised societies expand like never before, especially in the second half of the twentieth century. This has included progress on women's equality, as well as legal recognition (and increasingly also public acceptance) of sexual, ethnic and cultural minorities. Even where complications cropped up, emancipation remained a positive touchstone. Ulrich Beck, for example, in his theory of a second – reflexive – modernisation, noted a growing awareness of the risks created by society, but regarded the simultaneous weakening of institutional ties as a welcome expansion of freedom. Beck did concede that his concept of reflexive modernisation was open to 'anti-modern' deviations and could certainly be directed against universal modern values. In a world of growing resource conflicts, for example, it is by no means certain that society will agree on humane forms of distribution. The cynical or chauvinistic exclusion of those in need from access to food, security and other necessities remains an option for the powerful – as observed in the conflict over Ukrainian grain exports in the wake of Russia's invasion. Nevertheless, Beck placed his hopes in a risk-driven democratisation of modern societies through empowered citizens acting in the 'subpolitical' sphere; their reflexive freedom would expand the positive aspect of individualisation and complete the mission of the 'first modernity'.[29] The new social movements and pressure groups of Beck's cosmopolitan society operate on a global scale, expressing a reflexive risk awareness that – like the radioactive cloud from Chernobyl – knows no national borders. This second reflexive empowerment is seen as the completion of modernity.

Today, that hope has lost much of its sheen. Almost forty years after Beck's *Risk Society* came out,[30] we must admit that the subpolitical 'democratization of democracy'[31] has not been able to prevent the proliferation of risks in society.[32] Instead, the concrete social manifestations of the normative principle of emancipation have been recognised as a problem for the reflexive treatment of modernisation risks. Ingolfur Blühdorn in particular has drawn attention to this fundamental problem. In a logic of 'second-order emancipation',[33] subjects understand – and defend – exploitation as liberation. The 'old critical orthodoxy'[34] of sociology, he posits, clung to an understanding of emancipation whose concepts of freedom had lost their relevance. The 'counter-project of liberation',[35] Blühdorn argues, interprets this modernist critique as a reaction to alienation. What the critics forget is that the people themselves identify emancipation primarily with a consumerist lifestyle.

Blühdorn dismisses the talk of individual emancipation as an academic and activist distraction that ignores the way 'the market and consumption (even at the bottom end) have become the most important locus and mode of self-exploration and self-realisation'.[36] The modernist ideal of emancipation, he argues, offers the reflexive subjects of late modernity carte blanche for selfish individualism, but absolutely no motivation for sustainable ways of life based on reciprocity. A social criticism centred on personal emancipation will almost automatically be understood as legitimising wasteful lifestyles. Ultimately, he points out, the critique rests on precisely the order it supposedly criticises. In other words, critical orthodoxy systematically legitimises the normative precedence of individual self-realisation, rather than challenging it. My gas-guzzling Audi must stay on the road, even if the petrol comes from Putin's Russia.

So the sociologists of freedom are subject to unintended consequences of emancipation that turn their ideas on their head. Under the banner of realising the free, authentic self, for example, the personal is staged online, liked and hated on the social media platforms, even as their toxic promises leave millions of teenagers suffering from anxiety and depression.[37] With the *Dialectic of Enlightenment* adorning their bedside table, the prototypical subject of late modernity stares into their iPhone, searching for a cheap polyester costume for the next cosplay party, to be airfreighted from China within a matter of days. In contexts such as these, individualism and emancipation must be understood as drivers of society's existential problems – and thus as sources of vital questions concerning adaptation.

In the recent past, we have seen supposedly existential societal problems cited to force through specific forms of social adaptation. In particular, the pressure to 'adapt' to the decline of Keynesian welfare capitalism (widely discussed as the neoliberal turn), as propagated by economic, political and academic elites since the 1980s, has left critical sociology fundamentally sceptical towards the very idea of societal adaptation.[38] It tends to identify adaptation with the depoliticising strategies of neoliberalism ('There is no alternative,' as Margaret Thatcher famously said) and the 'great adaptation'[39] to the capitalist market. As this criticism correctly notes, the supposed lack of alternatives is a function of very concrete group interests rather than any real existential imperative. As Blühdorn argues, the neoliberal turn (the 'technocracy of adaptation'[40]) has increasingly shunted central political decisions into post-democratic formats (such as expert committees, central banks and international legal instances), while democratic processes have become largely simulative.[41] Here, the prime concern has been the survival of capitalism rather than the survival of the species.

In fact, the question of survival has been explicitly instrumentalised for economic interests under the banner of adaptation to climate change.[42] Contrary to the popular narrative that adaptation to climate change only rose to prominence after the failure of mitigation (in the sense of prevention), political economist Romain Felli demonstrates in his analysis of the coevolution of climate policy and the neoliberal turn that adaptation has been the decisive response of the capitalist elites to the discovery of anthropogenic global warming since the 1970s.[43] Initially it was argued that reducing global warming was technically unavoidable and adaptation was the only option. As economic cost-benefit modelling proliferated during the 1970s, the capitalist market came to be regarded as the solution rather than the problem. This was led in particular by economists such as Thomas Schelling, William Nordhaus, Mancur Olson, Jesse Asubel, Gary Yohe and Lester Lave. Their response to calls for state intervention 'operated at two levels':

First, they sought to relativise the climate problem, making it comparable to other economic questions: through cost/benefit analyses, the climate question could be treated not as a moral question but rather as a choice of how to allocate resources. Second, once climate policies seemed to have become an inevitability, the economists worked to ensure that these policies would conform, as far as possible, to the operation of the market. Together, these two responses implied the need to emphasise the theme of adaptation.[44]

Beck's proposition of a coevolution of personal self-realisation and societal development is contextualised in two respects by the capitalism-critical findings outlined above. Firstly, they underline the existence of a specific mode of capitalist economy behind the spiralling existential threats. Secondly, this capitalism-critical rejection of adaptation ultimately shares with Beck and the critical orthodoxy a perspective on the adaptive society that preserves modernity's primacy of individualism (although with a rather different framing). The theory of reflexive modernisation hopes to contain existential risks through a subpolitical subjectivity whose reflexivity gains are ultimately a product of successful individualisation – or in other words, self-realisation. The capitalism-critical perspective on adaptation, on the other hand, regards the narrowing of self-realisation to the sphere of the market as the real problem. Freedom, it would argue, lies outside of capitalism. And if capitalism declares adaptation an imperative, then adaptation is automatically part of the problem, not the solution. Thus, in their elevation of the ideal of emancipation, both share the normative frame of the critical orthodoxy described by Blühdorn.

My interest here is not to weigh one normative position against another. Instead, I want to underline that the perspectives laid out above fail to address the big existential questions at all. The perspectives of individualisation and self-realisation remain central here – whether as last resort (Beck) or normative backdrop (to critical orthodoxy and capitalism-critical stances). They all welcome any expansion of personal freedom and opportunity – despite the risks[45] – whereas a sober assessment would more likely identify individualism as a driver of existential threats.

The risk logic that was central to the original theory of reflexive modernisation can also be identified within critical sociology itself. We can distinguish three fields of existential risk that are fundamentally bound up with the capitalist ideal of individualisation. Firstly, we have the problems of making a living under capitalism, especially in connection with questions of social inequality. In economic terms, it is broadly acknowledged that we are experiencing a secular growth and stability crisis. In the early 1960s, it was assumed that the economy would grow uninterruptedly, and that the highly developed economies had transcended the economic cycle of boom and bust.[46] Today there is enormous uncertainty about the longer-term trends. In response to the persistent stagnation of growth since the 1970s, the financial sector became a central driver of efforts to renew and revive capitalism.[47] In order to secure their legitimacy amidst falling rates of growth, states had to find ways to continue to fulfil the expectations of material and social security that had become established in the context of the post-war boom.[48] This required capital, which was largely supplied by the financial sector. The private sector also hunted for innovations to revitalise a sclerotic economy. The financial sector itself turned out to be a crucial crucible of renewal. Its 'innovative' investment products promised levels of profit that were no longer possible in the 'real' economy.[49]

The financialised capitalism of our age only survives by consuming its own future, devouring its own economic and social foundations.[50] Debt has become a central factor since the 1970s,[51] as the economy successively lost its ability to generate growth by improving productivity and expanding markets.[52] In essence, debt allows capital to be sold before it has even been generated. The more money is created, the more future resources can be consumed in the present, presuming stability of the currency. This orientation on 'consuming the future' has gradually crept into other parts of the economy. It is a central mechanism in the commercial internet, as the most important growth area of the past twenty years.[53] But this increases the risk of acute crises, because doubts over future profitability propagate especially quickly under conditions of economic volatility and can bring investment crashing to a halt at any moment.

These efforts to stabilise capitalism have certainly led to a sharpening of social inequality and have exacerbated reproduction problems among the losers of the successive financial crises. For example many less-wealthy households in the United States lost all they owned in the 2008 subprime meltdown, while richer households' assets were more widely spread and better secured.[54] While all income groups suffered losses, the top earners recovered comparatively quickly,[55] while those on lower incomes were left fearing for their social existence. This pattern was then repeated during the Covid-19 pandemic, when the wealth of the biggest billionaires actually grew while millions fell into poverty.[56] Even without acute economic crises, the profits of the new capitalism are extremely unequally distributed. Despite a reduction in social inequality at the country level, the world's poorest and the lower strata in the rich countries have seen no gains since the late 1980s, while the wealth of the 'hyper-wealthy' quintupled in real terms between 1987 and 2013.[57]

Changes in the labour markets of the highly developed economies have further polarised the social structure. The tertiary and digital transformations have made knowledge the central driver of capitalist renewal,[58] alongside the traditional 'fictitious commodities' of labour, land and capital.[59] This has transformed production processes and education and labour markets in ways that make subjectivity a central source of value and place it at the heart of the restructuring. This created new opportunities for fulfilment that were unconstrained by sclerotic bureaucracy and industrial toil – in particular for highly qualified individuals.

But the rise of the 'cognitive-cultural' economy has placed new burdens and expectations on its subjects.[60] Credentialled expertise is often only half the battle. Highly personal characteristics like creativity, social skills, intellectual flexibility and reflexivity are also demanded. This new career profile is embedded in a culture that not only promises and rewards positive emotions and success but explicitly demands them.[61] Its paradigm is the 'entrepreneurial self',[62] exhibiting 'responsibility, initiative, flexibility, agility' and creativity, but also subject to 'compulsory creative self-realisation'.[63] Drawing on the work of Luc Boltanski and Ève Chiapello, we can understand this constellation as an outcome of the artistic critique formulated by the radical movements of the 1960s, which railed against the cold objectivity and uniformity of a male-dominated 'society of generality'[64] and saw new forms of self-realisation as a practical critique of power. This cultural revolution opened up opportunities for enormous sections of society whose advancement had been institutionally blocked. In the first place, this applied to women, but has become increasingly salient on the axes of sexuality and ethnicity too.

The ambivalent aspect of this innovation is glaringly obvious, as is the price of the associated emancipation gains. In the social structure, for example, the cognitive-cultural transformation of capitalism has opened up new divides. The rise of the university-educated, generally urban, service classes[65] has been accompanied since the 1980s by the emergence of a growing and politically volatile 'service proletariat',[66] for whom maintaining an acceptable standard of living represents a permanent challenge. In geographical terms, this sets the beneficiaries of transformation in the most dynamic conurbations against the 'losers of globalisation' in the former centres of heavy industry, who have in some cases suffered massive loss of status.[67] The 'status panic' identified in parts of the middle class ultimately represents fear for their ability to preserve their way of life.[68]

The imperative of self-realisation in cognitive-cultural capitalism represents a separate source of specific *subjective* existential problems. The crisis of subjective stability forms the second set of threats that plague the self-image of the adaptive society. This is the dark side of the cultural primacy of self-realisation (whereby the changing form of capitalism should be understood as an expression – rather than a cause – of the rise of autonomy and authenticity as defining cultural values). One illustration of the subjective reproduction crisis is the observed shift in psychiatric diagnoses in the course of the twentieth century, from neurosis to depression.[69] While neurosis is a 'sickness of guilt', depression is 'a *sickness of responsibility*'.[70] Its origin lies, as Alain Ehrenberg puts it, in the 'the weariness of the self'; the exhausting burden of having to be a special, unique individual. In many cases, the root causes of depression and burnout are personal experiences of disappointment, in particular personal failure to fulfil social expectations and requirements.[71] Because of its fundamental function in distributing opportunities, the capitalist market represents a prime source of such disappointments. Here, cultural values collide with social structures. Individuals are required to be ever more successful, unique, authentic and creative, while the market-driven society offers only a handful of them high-status positions, continues to demand functional conformity, and condemns many people to unrewarding menial labour. So the project of personal self-realisation through employment is frequently doomed to failure, and it is fortunate that society offers a growing spectrum of comparatively independent arenas of individualisation. If your work is unfulfilling, you can still become a popular football trainer, a talented karaoke singer or a recognised political activist.

Subjective problems arise where the channels of compensation are obstructed or blocked. It is no coincidence that burnout was first observed in the social and caring professions, whose practitioners tend to identify strongly with their highly demanding work.[72] That constellation creates obstacles to seeking compensation in other fields. Elin Thunman sees the combination of authenticity and altruism that is typical of the caring professions as a source of possible disappointments.[73] The risk, she argues, has been further heightened by the privatisation and competition that has infiltrated this sector since the crisis of welfare capitalism. Pressure to cut costs translates into pressure to work harder and longer, and makes it impossible to derive self-worth through external recognition of altruistic activities. If the time allowed for each patient or client is reduced, the personal aspect will inevitably fall by the wayside. What is left is the feeling of being unable to live up to one's own standards and losing hope of self-fulfilment. Their altruism places carers under permanent tension and encourages self-exploitation to the point of collapse: in other words, it endangers their subjective well-being.

These sociological perspectives on mental health bear a striking resemblance to older theories about the phenomenon of relative deprivation,[74] which attribute negative attitudes, states and actions to the experience of disappointed expectations. People believe that they are not getting what they deserve, either measured against cultural expectations or in comparison to relevant others. One student begrudges another's internship. Young academics are jealous of their older peers who 'had it so easy'. Established communities resent refugees who supposedly receive more from the state than they themselves do.

Whereas burnout and depression are experienced as personal problems, political sociology regards relative deprivation as a driver of social criticism and political rebellion,[75] especially when the disappointment is experienced collectively. From this perspective, the populist revolts experienced by liberal democracies[76] and the depressive exhaustion of the authentic subject are two sides of the same societal coin. Their common denominator in late modernity is the individual's inability to fulfil society's expectations.

Thirdly, after the socio-economic and subjective troubles, we come to the existential ecological problems. Capitalism has expanded massively since the end of the Cold War, with more than fifty countries opening up their economies to the capitalist market since 1989 (globalisation).[77] The confluence of three developments – the integration of eastern Europe into the global capitalist economy, the rise of China to become the factory of the world, and the creation of increasingly complex transnational value chains – opened up new geographies of capital accumulation, while natural resources were consumed in unprecedented volumes and with dramatic consequences. Capitalist development, which had always been extractive on the peripheries of the global system, meant the expansion of a resource-intensive mode of economy and way of life into these regions. The mass of resources extracted globally, for example, grew from 27 billion tonnes in 1970 to 92 billion tonnes in 2017, and with it the volume of greenhouse gas emissions.[78] Because the growing global demand for raw materials is largely served by low- and middle-income countries, the associated environmental costs are increasingly outsourced to those countries.[79] The expansion of agricultural land by 190 million hectares between 1960 and 2019 occurred entirely in the Global South,[80] while the total actually shrank a little in the Global North.[81] Agriculture was the primary driver of the loss of 420 million hectares of forest between 1990 and 2020 – principally tropical rainforest in Africa and South America – with dramatic consequences for the biosphere (extinction of species and loss of habitat).[82]

Economic shifts in the capitalist centres have not fundamentally changed the catastrophic ecological impact of global capitalism. The developed economies have certainly been transformed since the early 1980s, with clean computer workstations replacing dirty coal mines and blast furnaces, tourism displacing resource extraction, ephemeral data supplanting mass and material. While this trend saw the consumption of the distinction-seeking middle classes become more culturalised and sophisticated,[83] it did nothing for the environment outside the developed economies: much of the heavily polluting 'old' industries were outsourced and relocated to developing and middle-income countries. To return to the example of the automobile: never have motor cars been as individualised as they are today (even if the aforementioned variations in colours and wheels may appear rather modest to the distinction-seeking consumer). But this is plainly anything but a resource-saving way of life. There is absolutely no sign of change when it comes to the trend of inexorable growth in global car ownership, which is estimated to have doubled every twenty years since 1976.[84]

Nor do the supposedly 'ecologically light' goods and distracting wonders of digital cultural capitalism offer any solution.[85] They turn out to make the ecological problems worse rather than better, because the associated technological infrastructures consume enormous amounts of energy and resources.[86] The so-called rebound effects of digital technologies also come into play here. Increases in productivity immediately lead to more consumption and greater use of resources.[87] Instead of reducing exploitation of the natural environment, the process has simply been redistributed extremely unequally across the globe. Today the smelters and blast furnaces pollute the air in India and China rather than Duisburg and Sheffield. Europe is not drowning in its own rubbish – but only because it ships it to Asia on freighters burning heavy fuel oil, simply externalising the costs.[88]

The current climate discussions underline just how strongly contemporary society sees itself faced with existential ecological crisis. Present and future ecological risks are perceived as lying beyond the scope of human control to an unprecedented extent. The discussion about *tipping points* illustrates this especially clearly. A tipping point describes the moment (or threshold) where a complex system enters a new state from which it cannot return to its previous condition. If feedback loops are involved, the new state may be highly dynamic. The classic example is the prospect of global warming causing the Siberian permafrost to thaw. This would release methane, which is a powerful greenhouse gas, and could accelerate atmospheric warming to a point where stabilisation becomes impossible.[89] Runaway warming becomes a plausible threat. In other words, the existence of tipping points means that we cannot base our plans on the assumption that trends are linear. This implies a loss of control that was anticipated neither by the original theory of the risk society (where problems were managed on the subpolitical level), nor by older theories from the Cold War era – when the threat of nuclear annihilation was at least under *somebody's* control. The reflexive consciousness of late modernity appears to have lost faith both in the self-regulating power of nature and in human society's ability to calculate and control it.

This loss of control and expectation of collapse has inspired some to peer into the abyss. Jem Bendell formulates a heuristic of deep adaptation to (imagined) non-linear climate change. In his scenario 'dangerous and uncontrollable levels of climate change'[90] take important elements of the global ecosystem past tipping points and cause 'mass starvation, disease, flooding, storm destruction, forced migration and war', and ultimately 'inevitable collapse and probable catastrophe' – for which we must prepare. Bendell proposes 'four Rs' to guide adaptive praxis. To begin with, we must promote *resilience*. First and foremost, this means defining normative priorities, because resilience revolves around the question of which norms, values and practices a society wishes to preserve through a fundamental adaptive transformation. This brings us, secondly, to the question of *relinquishment*: 'people and communities letting go of certain assets, behaviours and beliefs where retaining them could make matters worse'. That might mean coastal settlements, particular forms of manufacturing or certain consumer products. Thirdly, *restoration* means rediscovering ways of doing things that industrial civilisation had otherwise abandoned or forgotten: rewilding, seasonal diets, communal ways of living. Finally, *reconciliation* with one another and with the inevitability of social collapse forms the fourth pillar of Bendell's deep adaptation, concentrating above all on survival in the face of massive loss and disruption.

Whatever one thinks of Bendell's arguments about the likely inevitability of collapse, his concept of deep adaptation exposes the deficits of certain criticisms of adaptation. For example, Bendell is impervious to the objection that adaptation is ultimately a vehicle of capitalist renewal. In his concept, the question of capitalism seems almost too trivial to address explicitly, and the social practice he proposes plainly has nothing in common with the capitalist dynamic. Similarly, the denunciation of adaptation as conformism appears trivial against the magnitude of the existential threats Bendell lays out. His visions of *restoration* inevitably involve embedding the individual back into the community – implying social forms that sociology associates with greater pressure to conform. At the same time, Bendell's adaptation is an experimental and transformative (rather than primarily repressive) practice, as other proponents of such strategies also emphasise.[91] The concrete manifestations of societal collapse remain vague. Sometimes he speaks of 'starvation, destruction, migration, disease and war'[92] as absolute determinants of the transition to post-collapse communities. Sometimes it is economic implosion, although this 'does not necessarily mean a complete collapse of law, order, identity and values'.[93] The possible societies conjured by such descriptions are worlds apart sociologically. Furthermore, 'starvation, destruction, migration, disease and war'[94] already define the existence of millions today – and even in the absence of strong left-wing politics, many would probably welcome the disappearance of capitalism (assuming the preservation of basic social structures). But it is certainly clear that Bendell's expectations amount to a catastrophe-driven transformation of industrial capitalism and the end of a society centred on individualism.

A radical emphasis on the existential – as exemplified by Bendell – allows us to construct an interpretation of the present that places our own concept of adaptation at the centre of social criticism. In such a practice, individual and collective adaptation coincide – as they do in hunter/gatherer societies – because adaptation is imagined not only as a necessary collective transformation, but as the only meaningful way of life. If sociology interprets these visions of adaptive practice as an expression of the consciousness of late modernity – which increasingly defines society more in terms of survival than self-realisation – we will also recognise the shift from personal prestige to collective transformation. The adaptive society plainly stands for more than just new burdens. There are also signs of new benefits. Ending the primacy of individual emancipation will allow the capitalist profit imperative, lifestyle stress and ecological guilt to fade away. At the same time, the primacy of survival generates its own problems of legitimacy because the focus on adaptation challenges more than just the concept of emancipation. It also means abandoning the paradigm of progress.

3. Modernity adé

> [I]t could be said that progress
> occurs where it ends.
> *Theodor W. Adorno (1969)*[1]

In the previous chapter we established adaptation as a central concept in late modernity. This plainly involves more than a critique of individualism. In fact, we are dealing with a new era – and a new relationship to time – that opens a door to adaptive ways of life. Classical modernism was essentially characterised by the idea that a society could and should create its own future. This represented a radical departure from the premodern religious frame, in which an all-powerful God governed people's fates for all eternity. To the post-Enlightenment liberal mind, the future was essentially a blank sheet on which the modern subject could – and should – draw whatever he (and occasionally she) wanted. New ideas about social organisation incorporated the real experience of the subjugation of nature to generate expectations of inexorable progress in the fields of science and technology, art, philosophy, ethics and society, and, importantly, advancement for humanity as a whole. The idea of striving for perfection became society's raison d'être.[2] From the eighteenth century, progress became a 'quasi-religious rallying cry'.[3] The combination of ideals of perfection with real advances in modernisation was simultaneously utopian and pragmatic.[4] The ideal of progress supplied incentives for industry in the here and now, working towards a chosen future. As such, progress became the watchword of the modern era.

Sociology has never been satisfied with merely observing these developments. As a genuinely modern discipline it is often (at least implicitly) committed to progress[5] – especially in the 'emancipatory sociologies'. Sociologists track improvements in social conditions (or their absence), noting any worsening of social inequality, discrimination and other problems and scouring social classes and protest movements for emerging forces of progress. At the theoretical level, critical sociology reflects on threats to progress and seeks possibilities to expand freedoms even in opposition to the zeitgeist. Even the gloomiest still need the emancipatory logic of freedom as the foil for their scenarios of loss and regression. A sociology that operates within those coordinates remains trapped within the frame of modernity: 'The story of decline offers no leftovers, no excess, nothing that escapes progress. Progress still controls us even in tales of ruination.'[6]

Nevertheless, the idea of progress remains central to critical analysis, without which its criticisms would be directionless. In other words, sociologists are attached to a construction that valorises their own role. They can see themselves as agents of change, laying out the theory for a practice that is dedicated to creating a better future. If sociology is not to be an entirely self-referential system, we must assume that society is responsive to its ideas. If the audience is to be inspired, it must at least be interested. But is that the case?

For some time now, sociological diagnoses have tended to suggest the opposite, pointing to a growing disaffection with the idea of progress. In particular, belief in historical progress is no longer a driver of political action. As long ago as 1982, the Shell Youth Survey found that a majority of young Germans (58 percent) took a dim view of the future.[7] Even the more optimistic among them expressed little or no hope for real improvement. They anticipated disaster and were prepared for the worst: environmental destruction, pollution, resource depletion, nuclear war, economic crisis and famine.[8] The study also found that the young people with the grimmest outlook were the most likely to be politically active and most motivated to resist the developments they feared. The authors suggested that the protest movements were rejecting the very idea of progress:

> [These young people] pursue politics rather like a fire brigade that knows (or at least suspects) that the fire can no longer be extin-

guished. They may be able to create a few firebreaks and rescue a handful of people, but the fire is still going to burn. Of that there is no doubt. ... Yet still they respond. And they do so without any expectation of fundamental political or economic change, without any hope of a political majority or revolution for real change. *This pragmatic optimism in the face of an apparently hopeless future sharply distinguishes the new protest movements from those of just a decade ago.*[9]

By 1981, the political avant-garde was no longer 'modern'. The youth had abandoned the idea of forging a better future, and that perception guided their political engagement. As the cited passage underlines, this led neither to dystopian uprising nor to doom-laden paralysis. Instead, we see a shift from the modern fixation on the future to a stance that is more concerned with survival in the present. This formed the decisive point of reference for a political praxis whose theme was now salvaging the future rather than shaping it. Rather than striding towards a shining dawn, the uppermost concern was now survival: *to ensure that there would be any future at all.*

Looking beyond the natural toing and froing of politics, that impression has only grown over time. The Shell Youth Surveys conducted since 2002 describe a 'pragmatic generation' that tends to focus on the present – in spite or because of their material insecurity.[10] Their utopias rarely extend beyond the present; what they desire is stability. Rather than striding into the future they want to preserve the present: ideally everything should stay as it is. Private happiness looms large. Personal advancement, personal relationships and personal recognition are their frame of reference, not social change.

The ice of political abstinence starts to thaw around 2015,[11] when interest in politics begins to grow again and a majority now see the future positively. This development is confirmed by the 2019 Shell Youth Survey, in which 52 percent said that they were optimistic about social developments, and 58 percent expected their personal life to improve.[12] However, a growing proportion also worry about climate change and its consequences for society's future. In other words, the key issues for the political avant-garde of this generation – articulated above all by the new climate movement (Fridays for Future) – are also reflected in the survey data.

Today, the young generation really does appear to be re-engaging with the big questions concerning the future of society, specifically global warming and the environment.[13] But they remain wary – to say the least – of the idea of progress. Their relationship to the future is predicated primarily on preserving the status quo. Instead of explicitly mapping out a desired future, their political activity revolves around securing a living and preventing catastrophe. But the ecological question has seen a shift in attitudes. Where the youth of the early 2000s retreated into private life, today's young generation has come back to the idea that the problems of society require collective responses. Like in the early 1980s, their political action is anything but utopian. Accepting the existence of real dystopia, their attention revolves around surviving the present. Now personal prospects are discussed as a question of collective practice.

Here we are dealing, it would appear, with a heightened risk awareness: any promise of a golden future must simply (and rightly) appear implausible. The origin of the observed rejection of progress lies in the emergence of a public debate around threats to survival.

It goes without saying that the nineteenth-century concept of progress is dead and buried. But even into late modernity, the idea that 'the future' might offer guidance in the here and now was still broadly accepted. The material basis was a still largely unbroken trust in the stability of the natural world – a luxury that appears thoroughly anachronistic today. The current generation is dealing with a future that has mutated from promise to threat (a process that is itself an effect of progress having become a problem). As already noted, the theory of reflexive modernisation understood the sense of crisis observed in the mid-1980s as an effect of real modernisation gains (i.e. progress).[14] Only if subjects were liberated from institutional constraints, Beck argued, would they be able to develop an awareness of the side effects and externalities of the modernisation process. This reflexive freedom was an effect of modern individualisation; renouncing it would ultimately open the door for anti-modern authoritarianism.[15]

From this perspective, the attitudes outlined above do not represent mistaken ideas (or false consciousness) that could be counteracted with a new, improved concept of progress, but rather a struggle with reality in the sense of seeking adaptation to real environmental conditions. In such a situation, preaching progress is simply futile – and for critical sociology, tantamount to denying its own diagnoses. Precisely the phenomena identified in sociological diagnoses of crisis – the socio-economic, subjective and ecological problems of the present time, in whose positive resolution neither the public nor sociologists themselves seriously believe – offer plausible causes for the observed rejection of progress. This represents a fundamental shift in timeframes. Just as the change from 'eternity' to 'the future' as the central point of reference characterised the modern relationship to time, the shift from 'future' to 'now' characterises the adaptive society.

Reflexivity implies heightened awareness of society's vulnerability to crisis, in the sense of the shift from individualism to survival, and is thus centrally relevant to adaptation.[16] It also explains the emergence and popularisation of new concepts relating to adaptation in academic, political and public debates. The concept of resilience has risen to prominence in this context since the 1990s. Its meaning has evolved over time, while its field of application has expanded enormously.

In material science, 'resilience' is associated with the flexibility and elasticity that allow a material to return to its original state after being subjected to strong external influences.[17] 'The future', in the sense of change of form, is suspended. The point is for the material to return to its temporarily endangered original state. The term's migration to the fields of psychology and social ecology – to which its contemporary popularity is attributable – reveals the idea of an assumed original state to be problematic. As applied to dynamic entities like individuals, groups and societies, resilience is primarily about preserving identities, socio-ecological equilibrium and social stability. Here, again, we are looking at a reflexive understanding of crisis rather than a positively connoted future.

In psychology, 'resilience' refers to the personal resources and abilities that people employ in order to cope with negative life events. Resilient individuals are less at risk of being dragged down by an unfavourable socio-economic environment or unbalanced by traumatic events. Resilient individuals are capable of recovering from shocks and growing with their challenges, and thus more adaptable to future stress situations. Change represents reactions to moments of crisis and preparation for future stress.

The normative connotation of resilience as a dynamic and fundamentally positive process of adaptation to unfavourable external circumstances[18] has spread from academic psychology into broader society. Its expressions include a multitude of commercial counselling applications, a flourishing advice literature, successful podcasts and individually tailored coaching. Perceptions of crisis popularise such offers. For example, resilience was a hot topic during the Covid-19 pandemic, especially in the discussions about the effects of lockdown on mental health.[19] Its aura as a central objective of personal development was boosted by psychological studies asserting that resilient individuals suffered less depression and anxiety during lockdown.[20]

In social ecology, on the other hand, resilience describes the complexity – and thus to an extent the unpredictability – of human-environment interactions at the systemic level.[21] The term was first used in this sense in the early 1970s to explain the stability of ecosystems in response to disturbance.[22] This made it possible to understand highly complex systems involving interactions at different temporal and spatial levels. This was the point at which humanity was first understood to be impacting ecosystems on a global scale. The models became more robust and reliable as they took account of fluctuations and gradually moved beyond the linear. This led to decisive advances in knowledge about real ecosystems. The idea that the behaviour of ecosystems could be reliably predicted and controlled was now abandoned. Instead, socio-ecological systems were expected to show unpredictable reactions and fluctuations and possess the ability to change and adapt. One objective of this strand of research is to enable decision-makers to enhance the resilience of socio-ecological systems in response to anthropogenic environmental impacts – for example, creating upstream flooding zones to protect cities or introducing new tree species that are better adapted to withstand climate change. Here, again, we find change functioning as an adaptive response to ensure stability. Securing survival (or preserving the present) represents the central objective of resilient social ecologies, with adaptive transformation playing a central role.

Sociology also discovered resilience, albeit much later.[23] The term became a new paradigm in the field of disaster and security research in the course of the 1990s, and found its way into national, supranational and transnational security policies.[24] The sociological aspect brings together the systemic perspective of social ecology and the individual perspective of psychology. In this context, resilience is understood first and foremost as protecting public infrastructure against disruption.[25] But individual citizens are also expected to contribute, for example by stockpiling emergency supplies. So resilience already stands for adaptation practices that are in certain respects based on the same combination of personal and collective effort that we have already identified as characteristic of a conceivable adaptive response to the contemporary crisis.

Wolfgang Bonß introduces an important distinction that helps us to understand the spectrum of resilient practices. He describes 'simple' resilience as concrete responses to past events, while 'reflex- ive resilience' defines practices that mobilise resources preventively, in anticipation of coming events.[26] In the context of climate change, *mitigation* represents a practice of reflexive resilience. Mitigation means creating and/or strengthening institutions, strategies and practices in an effort to cushion the impacts of a particular development, or ideally to prevent them altogether – for example, planting trees to limit desertification and loss of grazing land. It is not restricted to the climate context. Sending vaccination teams accompanied by social workers into disadvantaged neighbourhoods during a pandemic mitigates the spread of the virus; removing names and photographs from job applications mitigates structural discrimination.

Describing mitigation as a practice of reflexive resilience places it under the umbrella of adaptation practices and leaves it open to misinterpretation. In the context of climate discussions in particular, the two concepts are frequently (and wrongly) treated as mutually incompatible. While mitigation has been interpreted as tackling the causes of climate change (for example reducing CO_2 emissions by expanding electric mobility and green energy systems or absorbing CO_2 through afforestation), adaptation has been taken to mean simply coping with the effects – and accepting a tragedy that could actually still be averted. The fear is that speaking too soon about adaptation will undermine mitigation efforts and make the situation even worse. In political terms, this controversy seems to be largely behind us, probably because the empirical findings of climate research make it increasingly clear that even sweeping mitigation efforts cannot avert the need for massive changes to our ways of life. As well as the pressures generated by extreme weather events, mitigation practices themselves will inevitably require massive interventions in conventional lifestyles. For example, heating a home and running a car may become unaffordable, or afforestation may compete with other land uses.[27]

In sociological terms, that is beside the point. Reflexive resilience involves precautionary practices under a logic where persistent recurring crises are already very much baked in. It seeks above all to prevent the worst rather than turning the clock back or changing the game. No grazing land is won back from the desert, the disadvantaged housing estate does not become a leafy suburb, and reformatting job applications does not make racism go away. While mitigation in this sense does seek to ameliorate symptoms, it does so without any faith that the causes of crisis can really be prevented. As such, it embodies the shift in modern expectations that lies at the heart of this book. Acceptance of a degree of irreversibility is inherent to the practices of reflexive resilience. If it were really possible to avert trouble, one would be bound to do so, rather than simply watering down its impact. The modern illusion that 'anything is possible' is largely suspended here. Certain things cannot be undone. Some things we will have to live with, even if we can still influence the severity of the consequences. The future is no longer a blank sheet on which the modern subject can write whatever they want. It is dynamic, precarious, uncontrollable. But not impervious to action. What we are seeing is attempts to preserve the present by adapting to the future.

Mitigation creates a future without any need for progress. Instead, the point is to prevent the worst. As it transpires, reflexive resilience is not foreign to modernist thinking. The practice of mitigation seeks to protect the status quo through actions that are guided by risk calculations. The term suggests that adequate precautions based on accurate analysis can at least ensure a degree of stability in our natural and social environments. In other words, mitigation is a matter of the scientific management of insecurity. So the modern concept of managing risk remains the objective. And this leads to a scientification of insecurity, which is especially visible in global climate strategy. The ubiquitous premise that the two degree ceiling promises a 'manageable' path is symptomatic. Here, mitigation promises predictability through proactive interventions based on increasingly complex risk calculations. However, the precautionary function associated with mitigation is by definition oriented more strongly on the current status quo than on any kind of future progress. Adaptation is key to preventing further deterioration and preserving the positive aspects of the status quo. So, by implication, action is guided more by normative assessments of the present than by modernity's promises for the future. We are no longer striding towards a bright future. But resilient practices might at least preserve a few openings for self-realisation that would otherwise be lost. Another way to look at this would be to see mitigation as a bridge to adaptation.

Contemporary critical sociology takes a dim view of the rejection of progress described above (whether simple or reflexive). Its attitude to resilience is heavily coloured by the classical sociologists of freedom and vacillates between rejecting the concept as ideological and bemoaning its very existence. Adaptation programmes are criticised for blocking discussion of possible alternatives, essentially arguing that they are intellectual distractions from real and desirable forms of emancipation. That line of argument generally asserts that emancipation will enable individuals to make sensible, rational decisions, and that the prospect of a better future is central to the corresponding practice. A person liberated from alienation will not only freely give up their fancy car and foreign holidays, but develop an entirely new and better way of life. This school of sociology sees the rejection of a modern concept of progress as a cardinal error. In effect, this brand of sociology has dug its own grave: its own increasingly dramatic diagnoses of crisis have successively discredited the modern project of progress. Sociology itself has promoted this turn. Criticising a shift in ideas for which they are themselves responsible, these sociologists are scrabbling to prop up an outdated normativity rather than investigating the role of the rejection of modernity in shaping our coming society.

The upshot of this is digressions that seek – implicitly or explicitly – to defend the modern ideal of progress against the reflexivity of society. For example, subject-centred analyses do acknowledge the relevance of resilient practices, but view them with scepticism. Their take on adaptation verges on the denunciatory (in a form all too familiar from the modern sociologies of freedom). Methodologically, the bird's eye perspective of discourse analysis dominates, formulating far-reaching hypotheses about the changing nature of contemporary subjectivity. Investigations of the resilient subject revolve around resilience, adaptation and vulnerability, as concepts rooted in the biopolitics of neoliberalism.[28] They tend to be more interested in the implications of resilience discourses for subjectivation and the underlying power structures than in the actors' reflexive synthesis. In the tradition of Foucauldian biopolitics and governmentality studies, analyses of this kind focus not on the experienced impacts of resilient practices, but on the modes of subjectivation that normalise these practices and thus impress them into the structures of society. They seek to reveal the invisible power structures behind everyday routines. These theories at least imply that the subjectivation – as the process by which the subject internalises their conditions and is in turn shaped by them – must change if the prevailing conditions are to be overturned. This form of practice embodies their understanding of emancipation and progress.

That is the perspective on self-regulation of the resilient subject developed by political scientists David Chandler and Julian Reid and sociologists Ulrich Bröckling and Stefanie Graefe. Chandler and Reid place resilience in the context of adaptation and vulnerability in order to examine contemporary psychopolitics and its effects under the neoliberal regime.[29] Under the resilience dispositive, they argue, security is increasingly regarded as a mission to be accomplished by the citizen – rather than the responsibility of the state – with external threats reinterpreted as personal challenges. Offloading responsibility onto the individual in this way is supposedly the only way to deal with the threats and risks that arise in the highly complex societies of late modernity. This creates and promotes a subaltern subject who appears to act autonomously but is in fact always adapting to the dangers of their environment. Each and every personal choice must be carefully weighed (and potentially justified). The resilient subject is left to accomplish this alone, in the face of persistent guilt and self-doubt. This, Chandler and Reid argue, creates a mechanism of control that far exceeds the possibilities traditionally ascribed to the democratic state.

Chandler and Reid see the sustainability discourse as the midwife to this involuntarily resilient subject.[30] Its emphasis on the biological, they say, projects permanent threats to life. The acute compulsion to adapt that is inherent to the resilience discourse has a pacifying effect and functions to ideologically buttress existing social power relations. The resilient subject's heightened ability to adapt to dangers subverts the path of political action to change the world. In this understanding, adaptation is the opposite of transformation. What is needed, Chandler and Reid conclude, is a subject that is capable of achieving a state of enduring security without heed to their biological vulnerability. The crux of this unmasking of the resilience ideology is plainly an idea of progress that implies something that the reflexive subject simply cannot have: a state of absolute security.

Prominent German cultural sociologists point us in a similar direction, although with less emphasis on security and progress. Ulrich Bröckling, for example, shows how the resilience dispositive forces subjects to expand – more or less boundlessly – their ability to adapt to the unavoidable and unpredictable. The resilient subject will always be surviving crises and dealing with the disruption they cause, so it is only logical if they reject any positive talk about the future. The subject, he argues, is trapped in the treadmill of the present and denied the possibility to meaningfully structure their own biography.

Bröckling comes to a similar conclusion for social systems. Beyond a certain degree of complexity, he argues, social systems must be exposed to danger if they are to survive. Promoting resilience means expanding the options for dealing with plausible threats – which are thus essential for the system's development. In the context of resilience, Bröckling reinterprets adaptation as opportunity. Although he does concede that programmes promoting resilience in pedagogical and even social-ecological contexts could certainly convey useful information, he points out that they would tend to offer a particular understanding of reality rather than concrete guidance for action. This, he argues, would offer a positive framing for the negative associations of risk prevention.

Other authors have already abandoned hope. Stefanie Graefe takes an analysis of burnout as the starting point for her critique of the resilience discourse. She asks what forms of autonomy might promote a governmentality of resilience and argues that the resilience dispositive tends to normatively reinforce and practically concretise practices of self-organisation and self-regulation (individual responsibility) rather than promoting autonomy. It is therefore no coincidence, she argues, that practices of resilience are associated in the first place with addressing personal trauma and seeking post-traumatic growth and development.[31] The autonomy of the resilient subject consists in gaining a more positive perspective on crises and the possibilities for overcoming them, accepting the changes and pursuing one's own goals. The promise of happiness through resilience normalises the idea of a satisfied, authentic life immune to disruption. Graefe criticises the way this pathologises states that were not previously regarded as abnormal.[32] She challenges Bröckling's interpretation of 'Homo resiliens' as a regressive variant of his 'entrepreneurial self'.[33] Instead, she argues that the resilient individual represents a form of subjectivation that is more about self-preservation than any entrepreneurial logic of self-realisation.[34] We should maximise meaning rather than utility, promote flexible development over linear growth, she says. Graefe aptly identifies resilience as a kind of reality shock,[35] confronting the entrepreneurial self with the consequences of capitalist crisis – and thus injecting reflexivity into the late modern ideal of progress.

According to Graefe, resilience dispositives hinder the emergence of stances critical of the status quo (as did the modern critical orthodoxy). Indeed, she warns against reinterpreting resilience as emancipatory. Like Bröckling, she regards the resilient self as a master of adaptation, but one that is at risk of becoming embroiled in fictitious threat scenarios. Paranoid anticipation supplants positive imagination. The family garden is no longer a place for leisure and relaxation, but a totem of self-sufficiency if supply chains collapse. In the city, there is danger round every corner, few pleasant surprises, never freedom. Rather than pursuing conformity and stability under resilience dispositives, Graefe concludes, the point is precisely not to fit in, but instead to attack the human conditions that cause crisis in society. In the modern dichotomy between emancipatory progress and adaptive stability, it goes without saying that strong, resilient subjects are needed.

Terms like *resilience* and *mitigation* thus define a post-progressive condition that has long been present in contemporary society. The associated sense of crisis demands action – not out of any expectation of progress but through an awareness of vulnerability. The writing on the wall might appear paranoid, but climate science and sociology are not exaggerating. What might at first glance look like a 'discursive strategy of depoliticisation'[36] reappears in this light as a reflexive attitude towards plausible expectations of crisis. Sociologists' reservations about rejecting progress appear negligible against contemporary empirical trends. Rejection of progress does not cause political paralysis or lack of ambition. Instead, adaptation opens up spaces where ways of life can survive that would otherwise be lost. The critique of resilience even recognises that concern for survival can engender criticism of capitalism.[37]

Similarly, the widely observed insistence on individual responsibility can only function as a mechanism of power in isolation from collective activity. But if it is true that the imperative of survival will promote both personal politics and collective action in the coming society, adaptation cannot be the repressive social practice denounced by the sociologists of freedom. Instead, it opens up a field of social struggles that lie largely outside the modern semantics of progress. The question is no longer how to achieve a fair distribution of growing economic prosperity, social entitlements and individual liberties, but how best to husband fundamentally scarce resources (be they raw materials, other environmental goods, economic profit or subjective capacities). Conflicts over values are also unavoidable, for example between solidarity and exclusion. Who to prioritise during a pandemic? The old who raised us or the children for whom we are responsible today? Who deserves our solidarity? The Ukrainians whose country was invaded or the pensioners who can no longer afford to heat their homes? Here we enter the field of adaptive conflicts: these are real conflicts over real sacrifices.

The modern semantics of progress has little or nothing to offer here. In the Aristotelian tradition, questions of survival lie outside the political process, given that biological reproduction occurs in the private household (*oikos*). That division of spheres collapses when survival is at stake – as seen in collective crises like the Covid-19 pandemic. It is thus no accident that Andreas Reckwitz concludes that the immediate health emergency of Covid-19 underlined the need for adaptation practices to be seen in a more positive light: anticipating negative futures can help us to develop long-term strategies. Reckwitz, who is otherwise closely aligned with the cultural sociologists discussed above, goes as far as to describe this learning process as 'society growing up',[38] treating resilience as a collective political praxis.

Reckwitz plainly does not want to abandon the idea of progress entirely, even if he steers clear of the 'classical maxims of modernity ... – freedom, prosperity, emancipation – and the belief that society can be shaped'.[39] Instead, he attempts to reconcile adaptation and progress. Stability and resilience are not ends in themselves, he argues. We need positive visions for society: 'a politics that transcends risk minimisation, a politics with positive ambitions to improve society, whether the ultimate objective is autonomy, prosperity, justice or sustainability'.[40] As the quote underlines, Reckwitz's understanding of progress is unteleological. He is not seeking to define ultimate objectives for the political or personal sphere. Instead, he understands progress as a mode of contingency opening (which in the context of resilience should balance contingency closure). Experimentation should certainly not be sacrificed at the altar of security.[41]

Reckwitz would like to see sociology tackle loss as 'the flip side of progress'.[42] Experience of loss is the taboo of a modernity whose 'social praxis' has consistently been characterised by 'the model of normative improvement'. On the other hand, he says, ignoring and potentiating loss is part and parcel of the modernisation process. If Tesla builds a factory on the outskirts of Berlin, this brings progress to the region in the form of state-of-the-art electric cars and thousands of badly needed jobs. Who cares about the scruffy woodland that has to be clear-felled, apart from a few local dog walkers? Or the groundwater, which Elon Musk claims is bountiful while his company drains it away? The old must make way for the new. And, as Reckwitz notes, if modernisation means permanent renewal through innovation, rationalisation, democratisation, acceleration and economisation, irrevocable losses are unavoidable. One could say that, under this premise, contingency opening – for example the career opportunities Tesla creates in the region – forms the functional substitute for experienced losses. In other words, any progress that occurs in such a context should be understood above all as a promise of personal advancement offering solace for what has been lost.

However, Reckwitz sees the problem of loss exacerbated in late modernity, in the 'combination of heightened sensibility to loss and escalation of loss'.[43] Today, when everyone knows that woodland and water are finite resources, any threat is directly affect-provoking and politicisable. Escalation of loss means escalation of our experience of loss, more so than in earlier phases of modernity. Reckwitz cites the popularity of narratives of doom as evidence for his theory: the death of democracy, the end of liberalism, galloping social inequality, the loss of social mobility, and so on. Sensitisation to loss, on the other hand, means first of all the loss of 'repression of loss' in the context of fading enthusiasm for progress. Here, Reckwitz puts his finger on changes in the modern zeitgeist that are reflected in a general reflexive caution. The people are not enthused. Not by vote-seeking politicians promising a gleaming future with high-tech jobs and electric cars, nor by career coaches and financial gurus who peddle much the same on social media. Reckwitz regards this partly as an effect of a culture that treats 'experiences of loss, sadness and pain' as subjectively relevant and socially acceptable. It is okay to be sad these days. We no longer need to fake a grin for every mention of progress. Now experiences of loss are articulated, without being drowned out by a rigid collective narrative of progress.[44]

The problem thus revolves around a highly subjectivised concept of progress. While hope for improvements in the broader social situation have gone thoroughly out of fashion (or society has abandoned progress), personal betterment is still on the agenda. We are left with just one side of the coin. Moreover, the idea of progress is internalised and frequently experienced negatively, as a discrepancy between elevated expectations of personal fortune and a hard reality that inevitably contradicts them.[45] To top it all, positive contingency opening can only begin after the existential problems have been resolved. But if survival (in the context of the adaptive society) becomes the crux of subjective meaning it must be expected that wishes for contingency opening will gradually fade away. Elon Musk is not only building factories in Berlin-Brandenburg and Shanghai but planning to colonise Mars. That might offer him a small degree of (subjective) contingency closure in relation to climate catastrophe – which he claims his electric cars will help to avert.

This 'halved' concept of progress in late modernity may have stabilising and structuring effects on personal perspectives. But 'progress' is no paradigm for societal responses to existential crises. In our new situation, hoping to 'mend' the idea of progress is about as useful as wishing for a return to a simple pre-reflexive modernity. From a reflexive perspective, the disenchantment of modernity actually represents the lifting of a veil. Rejecting progress enables us to encounter the world with an adaptive sense of reality and promises liberation from responsibility for a project that has lost its credibility. In the age of survival, we are no longer talking about the self-regulating powers of modernity, but only the self-stabilisation of an adaptive society. Like it or not, sociology is going to need to take that on board.

4. Adaptive rebellion

Listen to science!
Fridays for Future

For all the criticisms of emancipation and progress laid out above, the existential imperative offers its own perspectives of freedom, in the sense that the adaptive society promises relief from the impossible dictates of late modernity by rejecting the tyranny of progress. I am certainly not arguing against freedom per se.[1] But abandoning the modern ideal can also be understood in positive terms, as an effect of reflexivity rather than bending to the (possibly internalised) social milieu. The contemporary sense of crisis is ultimately enlightening and reflects a specific desire for meaning drawn from the adaptive life itself. What would a society that rejects the ideal of progress look like? What ways of life would it involve? What kind of 'good life' can a truly adaptive society offer?

Those questions, to which I now turn in the remaining three chapters, could fill an entire research programme on life in the adaptive society. The details – from resilience coaching and quasi-religious teachings to resonance theory[2] and reciprocity – undoubtedly merit sociological exploration in their own right. But that path leads quickly into the weeds, and would distract from the broader picture I am seeking to draw. Instead, before moving on to examine a slice of empirical evidence in Chapter 5, I would like to outline two important theories of adaptation. These are Marshall Sahlins's observations on life in societies that had no concept of progress and Robert K. Merton's challenge to the idea that adaptation means conformity and obedience. If we are looking to explore adaptation as a positive praxis that can create opportunities and expand individual and collective freedoms, we need to consider how societies might function without modernity's imperative of progress. Given that we can only speculate about the future, we had better start with a look back at the past.

Affluence and *prosperity* were the watchwords of the 1950s and 1960s.[3] After the hardships of the first half of the twentieth century, Western societies now placed a premium on economic growth and consumer goods for the masses. John Kenneth Galbraith's highly influential *The Affluent Society* (1958) laid out the Keynesian case for government investment in infrastructure and a strong welfare state to eliminate poverty.[4] Ludwig Erhard, who led West Germany's 'economic miracle', proposed 'prosperity for all'.[5]

This discourse was challenged by ideas emerging from the counterculture of the sixties. Setting aside the conventional fixation on the production and distribution of goods and services, they turned critical attention to the question of what affluence really means. This turned out to be particularly productive where alternative frames of reference cast a new light on modernity and its obsession with progress. In the 1960s, for example, anthropology witnessed a debate over the question of affluence in the context of human ways of life before the advent of sedentism and agriculture.

In 1966, a young cultural anthropologist named Marshall Sahlins made waves with his concept of an 'original affluent society'.[6] Hitherto, it had been widely assumed that hunter-gatherer societies had barely scraped a living. Incapable of generating any meaningful economic surplus, they had lived from hand to mouth, always on the brink of starvation. Sahlins pointed to evidence that certain groups of hunter-gatherers had been able to satisfy all their needs directly from their environment. And because their needs were modest and demanded relatively little labour, they were able to live a life of abundance – in particular with respect to time. Sahlins's hunter-gatherers easily found the little they needed. They savoured their free time – with leisure and feasting – rather than performing unnecessary additional work.

The attraction of this concept (apart from its obvious appeal to teenagers) lay principally in a way of life very different from the 'white heat of technology'. Sahlins explicitly challenged the doctrine of economic scarcity,[7] which treats access to fundamentally scarce goods as the driver of all human activity. People, he argued, have not always wanted more than they can get.

From a sociological perspective, the economic motivation is characteristic of capitalist modernity. Modern societies generate compliance[8] by promising that discipline will be rewarded with access to economic goods. Those who fit in and knuckle down can expect their tiny slice of society's cake. Adaptation is key here. If you want to join the game, you have to play by the rules.

Ultimately, this mechanism of 'dynamic stabilization'[9] offers little more than trivial pleasures and technological distractions. Its brand of freedom boils down to the choice between McDonald's or Burger King, Apple or Android. Where the economist sees only eternal human nature, a sociologist would point out the desire for deeper meaning. In this scheme of things, the individual's actions in the here and now are guided by a yearning for progress, for a better future. Scarcity is the foundation of the entire edifice.[10]

Sahlins's hunter-gatherers had no concept of scarcity. They had no unbounded desires and lived largely in the here and now. Desiring little, their wants were 'easily satisfied'.[11] All the same, they did have to adapt to changes in their environment. A particular source of food might appear only seasonally or become depleted. Hunter-gatherers were by necessity nomadic, moving on as their material needs dictated. And that in turn predicated frugality, to the point of an aversion to extraneous material possessions. Everything had to be carried. Superfluous portable goods restricted their mobility, while fixed property had to be left behind and was essentially worthless. This way of life mitigated firmly against any accumulation of material objects. Instead, as long as their minimum subsistence was ensured, their acceptance of limits enabled them to adapt their needs and way of life.[12]

The hunter-gatherers were not seeking a better future, but maximising their free time in the present. This is not the driven, progress-seeking existence of the modern age. Sahlins suggests that they were able to fulfil their material needs with five hours of daily work. A skilled craftsman might spend 'most of his time talking, eating and sleeping'.[13] As far as Sahlins was concerned, the transition from the hunter-gatherer existence (which represents 90 percent of human history[14]) to agriculture (with seasonal crop storage and accumulation of surpluses) must have been a process of violent enforcement, given that it abolished a situation of abundance and replaced it with an order where ordinary people had to work harder. That cannot have been attractive to Sahlins's hunter-gatherers.

Sahlins discusses the hunter-gatherers' 'adaptively stabilised'[15] way of life as the explicit opposite of hierarchical society and in particular industrial modernity. His 'original affluent society' demonstrates the possibility of a way of life where 'progress' actually meant doing without the modern regimes of time and value. Instead of describing the hunter-gatherers as *poor* because they own nothing, Sahlins argues that they should be regarded as *free* – for exactly the same reason. This introduces a specific understanding of freedom based on agency in the here and now (rather than in some spiritual otherworld or abstract set of rights).[16] Everything they gathered and hunted had to be consumed more or less immediately. Just as material goods restricted mobility, food storage was regarded as unnecessary and in fact counterproductive. Sahlins notes that the original affluent society had no problem with 'low productivity of labor'. But their 'economy' was 'seriously afflicted by the imminence of diminishing returns',[17] in the sense that the harder they worked to increase their material possessions, the harder it became to reproduce their way of life.

Sahlins's theory has been widely discussed and debated in the interim, and there are certainly details that needed to be revised and corrected.[18] But Sahlins was plainly also commenting on the narrowness of the economic debates of the 1950s and 1960s and proposing an alternative critique of capitalism.[19] For present purposes, we are especially interested in the 'good life' lived by his hunter-gatherers. This is a concept of freedom that challenges entrenched ideas about property and power, predicated on an adaptive way of life to which the modern idea of progress is entirely foreign.

This way of life is opportunistic rather than conformist. Interestingly, 'opportunism' is another concept that is derided in the modernist canon. In fact, all it means is taking chances that are offered under given conditions. In this original sense, adaptation means seeking out opportunities and following the simple priorities of survival. You use what you find, saving time and energy by keeping things simple.

The way of life described by Sahlins existed within narrow limits. The cycles of nature were stable; time was flat and unhistorical. Changing the world was not a concern of human activity, and the fearsome engine of 'civilisation' had yet to roar into life. Moreover, adaptation occurred in a framework where expectations were relatively dependable – and very different from today's.

The question of progress only arises in a dynamic society in which diverging expectations about the future compete with one another as political ideologies. One central heuristic here is Karl Mannheim's three native ideologies of modernity and their different perspectives on the future.[20] Liberalism regards the future as a blank sheet, socialism ties it to liberation, while conservatism seeks to preserve cultural difference into the future. Despite their different perspectives, all three see the future as a special preserve: of the liberal individual, of a historically predestined class, or of a particular cultural community.

As well as offering growing opportunities for individualisation and self-realisation, modernising societies are naturally also subject to conflicts, tensions and pressure to adapt. Over time, these traits are recognised as both imminent to the society and challenging to the individual. Yet there is little in the way of sociological theory that recognises adaptation as a positive, flexible and explicitly *transformative* praxis.[21] The theory of adaptation developed in the 1930s by Robert K. Merton represents an important exception.

Merton's starting point is the existing social order, in which adaptation is the norm. He is interested in social change and everyday responses to crisis. Merton's analysis of adaptation as a potentially transformative praxis builds on the work of Émile Durkheim, who pioneered the understanding of anomie as normlessness and social disintegration.[22] Durkheim describes anomie as an unbalancing of the social order and locates its causes in the disruptive effects of modernisation. Merton also regards anomie as inherent to modern society, seeing it as a constant side effect of gradual social change. Pressure to adjust is thus universal and fundamentally systematisable. As such, Merton connects adaptation primarily with conformism (sometimes positively connotated, sometimes negatively). Merton's adaptation is a flexible, even creative praxis.

Merton explores the social roots of deviance in his seminal essay 'Social Structure and Anomie' (1938), where he identifies two central aspects: Firstly, what sociology at the time defined as deviant or abnormal behaviour was in fact largely a praxis of adaptation; secondly, these practices are the outcome of social constellations that place subjects in impossible situations. The clerk who appears strangely distracted and incapable of applying any personal initiative to his bureaucratic tasks does not do so because there is something wrong with him personally. The school student who devotes her energy to successful cheating is not necessarily morally delinquent. Instead, Merton shows how such problems are created by the gap between culturally prescribed objectives and the means available to achieve them. His distinction between *culture* and *society* points to tensions that individuals handle in different ways.

The clerk, for example, rigidly adheres to administrative rules – to the detriment of the organisation – because he sees no personal perspective in his work. He is denied promotion, ignored by his boss and rejected by the colleague he would like to flirt with. The cultural goals he expected to pursue through his work – career, recognition, social integration – are unachievable. Society's rules are to blame. Promotion requires a qualification he will never have, while his boss treats him as a function rather than a person, and his colleague knows that workplace relationships are frowned upon. His recourse is to conduct his work in an exaggeratedly formal manner. Merton describes this as adaptation to the erosion of particular cultural values; today one might call it 'coping'. But he does not give up. His cranky attitude is but a symptom of his adaptive 'ritualism'.[23]

The school student is a different matter. She wants to be successful. Good marks mean achievement, praise and perhaps extra pocket money. What she does not believe in is the rules that govern her success. Her problem is not with the dominant cultural values (in this case, success) but with the means society grants her to achieve it. Merton recognises this as a typical and absolutely realistic perspective of the lower social classes. They know that games are won by those who are quick to grasp the explicit and implicit rules. Those are – as any educational sociologist would confirm – the others. The school student sees no alternative to bending the rules if she is to achieve her goals. Her strategy of adaptation is 'innovation'.[24]

Alongside ritualism and innovation, Merton describes three further modes of adaptation: conformism, retreatism and rebellion. While critical theory understands conformism as the forced adaptation experienced by the powerless, Merton's reading casts it in a different light. As he points out, the conformist must be able to afford to conform in the sense of both embracing cultural goals *and* possessing the means to achieve them. In this sense, it is the typical attitude of those who profit from the status quo. Retreatism, by contrast, is the ultimate outsider practice. A person who rejects the norms and values of a specific culture and stands outside its institutions is, strictly speaking, no longer part of society. Merton identifies this mode of adaptation with 'psychotics, psychoneurotics, chronic autists, pariahs, outcasts, vagrants, vagabonds, tramps, chronic drunkards and drug addicts'.[25]

Rebellion, finally, is the mode of adaptation of the rising classes. In Merton's words, 'It is typically a rising class rather than the most depressed strata that organizes the resentful and the rebellious into a revolutionary group.'[26] This is the most dynamic of the five modes of adaptation, standing not only for rejection of the existing culture and society but for implementation of the new. Merton distinguishes rebellion from resentment, which he interprets as an aggressive form of innovation whereby values are maintained, but the rules are applied aggressively (the state should take care of the poor – and deport the refugees).

Unlike the founders of critical theory, Merton is not thinking about adaptation to rigid power structures. His interest is adaptation in the context of social change experienced as crisis. Under this perspective, adaptation is diverse and even creative. It can be a strategy for personal salvation – or a praxis of collective awakening.

Adaptive generations

So can we apply this typology of adaptation to today's society? Is there any sign of positive, creative approaches to the crises facing us today? According to the theories outlined above, we should be looking for these among groups that are addressing the root causes of the problems, operating as agents of social change, and advancing adaptive programmes. Merton points us to the 'rising classes' as the standard-bearers of rebellion. We need to understand this in the context of modern industrial society, where questions of affluence and class are so central. His term 'rising *classes*' suggests conflict over resources, opportunities and progress. Do 'rising classes' offer any perspective for today's pressing questions of survival, or do we need to look for other actors? If we begin empirically, by considering who is already rebelling against the crises, we find ourselves looking at generations rather than social classes.

While there is a tendency to project characteristics onto entire generations, sociologists tend to be more interested in generational *elites*. These are often comparatively smaller groups that are perceived (especially retrospectively) as the political voice of their generation. Generation and class each play a role in social transformation. Karl Mannheim's understanding of generations combines natural and social time: it is the social aspect of the biological cycle of birth and death that enables the renewal and transformation of society.[27] As Heinz Bude notes: 'An assertive generational consciousness is part and parcel of a dynamic world, looking to the future and striving for renewal. It breaks with the known and familiar to enable the new, the unknown and unfamiliar.'[28] In the second half of the twentieth century, that dynamic shaped the cultural project of liberalisation and individualisation. In Germany, for example, the 'new social movements' of the 1980s have been described as 'engines of modernisation'.[29] Dissecting the French example in their influential investigation of the 'new spirit of capitalism', Luc Boltanski and Ève Chiapello identify the artistic critique of the 1960s as the driver of a restructuring of industrial society, seeking to expand the opportunities for self-realisation.[30] Those generations were dedicated to progress and emancipation. By the 1980s, the dreams of the youth had turned to nightmares.

If we apply these concepts to the present day, we can identify specific qualities in the current protest generation that mark out its members as possible agents of rebellious and transformative adaptation. First of all, the heart of the current wave of climate protests (especially the Fridays for Future movement) is a demographic that could quite plausibly turn out to represent a generational elite.[31] The idea of a 'rising' group, which Merton associated with class in industrial society, applies here too – in a generational sense where the young are always the rising cohort of the coming period. In the case of the new climate movement, it is the (future) educated elites who are powering the protests. The movement initiated by Greta Thunberg (who was herself just fifteen years old at the time) is overwhelmingly young, largely female and heavily skewed towards the more educated.[32] Surveys of Fridays for Future participants in Bremen and Berlin in 2019 found that the 14-to-19-year-olds were by far the largest cohort (51.5 percent) followed by the 20-to-25-year-olds (19 percent).[33] School and university students where one or both parents themselves have a university education were strongly overrepresented in the FFF demonstrations. The participants' perceptions concerning class were equally telling: 63.4 percent said they were upper middle class.[34] Similar patterns are found internationally. Mattias Wahlström and his colleagues conducted field research at FFF protests in thirteen European countries and found the preponderant age cohort to be the 14-to-19-year-olds (45 percent).[35] They also confirmed that overrepresentation of participants from highly educated families is an international phenomenon. A total of 72.3 percent of their surveyed school students reported that at least one of their parents was a university graduate. So this is a movement that is generationally and socio-structurally predestined to arrive in the upper echelons of society.[36]

Here, we also see the confluence of natural and social time that typifies generations. The climate activists feel that their biological youth lends them a special right to speak about the future – which they will experience but older generations will not. At the same time, natural time – which is now characterised by the crisis of the planetary ecosystem – becomes a problem for the protestors' social time. The movement's belief that the environment is severely out of kilter precludes any talk of progress – which assumes the natural world to be external and stable – and politicises intrinsically personal questions of survival. Who wants to say the future belongs to the young when we are apparently all going to hell in a handcart?

That, it seems, is actually one of the aspects that define this generation. The generational elites of modernity were shaped by intense shared experiences such as war and depression that coloured their subsequent understanding of society. The youthful climate protests are very clearly motivated by the anticipation – rather than experience – of grief. The 'children of the apocalypse'[37] see a dystopian future and are mobilised by the existential threat. For the climate movement, the question is not *how* the future will look but *if* it will happen at all.[38]

This time around, the generation is defined by expectation rather than experience. And a measure of reflexivity is observed. Acting on future catastrophe is no trivial exercise. Most people don't even try. Ideas about progress are almost completely absent from the movement's demands. If progress is mentioned at all, it is in the context of progress towards climate neutrality by 2030. Here, progress is nothing but 'an answer to the doubt and the hope that things will finally get better, that people will at last be able to breathe a sigh of relief' (Theodor W. Adorno).[39]

The movement's ideas about the future are correspondingly modest and revolve largely around the imperative of collective survival. The 1.5 degree target must be met at any cost.[40] If it is not, they say, the consequences for humankind and the natural environment will be catastrophic. Questions of self-realisation look very different under the primacy of survival. For example, Luisa Neubauer and Alexander Repenning, two prominent leaders of the German Fridays for Future, write about 'the luxury of riding a bicycle'[41] as a life choice that combines freedom of movement, ecological transport and control of time. They contrast this with the false freedom of a highly individualised 'fossil' lifestyle. Self-realisation trimmed for survival tends to follow the maxim that 'small is beautiful'[42] rather than the extensive logic of progress (maximising consumption and productivity). It requires us to remember that natural resources are finite, and we should use them responsibly in harmony with the animate and inanimate world. That perspective is not so far from the 'Zen road to affluence' followed by Sahlins's hunter-gatherers.[43]

Alongside its survival paradigm and rejection of progress, a third feature of the movement's output also points to a constellation of adaptation: its political programme makes no distinction between individual and collective change. Even if the climate movement has been trying to move beyond personal moralising to advance a broader politics, most of its activists are well aware that both tracks are required: climate-motivated action by individuals and action by governments and businesses to promote and institutionalise the actions of individuals. To consume responsibly and to hold businesses responsible. To buy second-hand clothes and boycott plastic bags, while also introducing supply chain legislation to regulate the fast fashion industry and its sweatshops.

The new climate movement could be seen as the political spearhead of an essentially adaptive way of life – emphasising survival, renouncing progress, and combining individual and collective praxis. It has taken flak from the left for its lack of imagination in developing alternatives.[44] In this respect, it could be seen as a classic risk movement, as the bearer of a subpolitical challenge to representative democracy that has been bubbling since the 1980s. In other words, it functions as a pacemaker of democratisation.

That interpretation skates over a peculiar characteristic that is rather at odds with the democratisation dynamic. At least in its public presentation, the new climate movement exhibits an extraordinary confidence in experts. As Ingolfur Blühdorn argues, that 'positivistic perspective is devoid of any memory or awareness of the decades of discussion about the subjective core of all supposedly objective science, or of the responsibility shared by experts who claim a monopoly on objectivity for the sorry state of contemporary society'.[45] This is pithily summed up in the slogan 'Listen to Science!' and manifested in the movement's close relationship with the 'Scientists for Future'. For our present purposes, it is irrelevant whether we regard this as naive or strategic.[46] Seen in connection with the movement's enthusiasm for a strong state,[47] it amounts to the rudiments of a political vision – ultimately a vision of depoliticisation. Essentially it boils down to an evidence-based technocracy, seeking to remove questions of survival from the arena of political conflict and democratic deliberation.

The visionary Ulrich Beck saw this coming in the 1990s. The inflation of subpolitics, he wrote, could end up hampering political and administrative agency by creating a 'congestion' that would massively obstruct political progress.[48] Applied to the present case, that would mean that the depoliticisation sought by the adaptive generation represented a response to frustrated expectations. Existential questions need to be solved. They *must* be solved. Real existing democracy has not exactly covered itself with glory, despite decades of subpolitical dynamisation (civil society). From the movement's perspective, it has exhibited the kind of political/administrative paralysis that Beck described as a 'congestion'. Today's civil society activism, which ultimately includes FFF, finds itself frustrated by its own success, with a subpolitically blocked democracy apparently unable to implement the decisions required for survival within the necessary timeframe. In that light, the positive technocracy of the new climate movement can be best understood as an attempt to accelerate the political in response to an apparently inevitable survival crisis – rather than a desirable resonance with nature, which Hartmut Rosa describes as medio-passive.[49] A positive concept of adaptation would mean switching the cultural reference from personal growth to collective survival and challenging the rules that govern society. Today, adaptation is rebellion.

5. Criticality and critique: The avant-gardes of adaptation

> Without collaborations, we all die.
> *Anna Lowenhaupt Tsing (2018)*[1]

The new climate movement has generated an *ecological critique*, exploring ways of life centred on survival.[2] This is just the latest in a long line of modernist criticisms of social conditions, whose roots lie in the nineteenth century and are closely associated with the native ideologies of the industrial age.[3] The socialist movement brought forth a *social critique* whose topics still reverberate today: class power, capitalist exploitation and social inequality. Its normative foundations are the value of labour and the desire for economic and social equality. The *artistic critique* is essentially liberal. It objects to mediocrity and uniformity, the alienation and authoritarianism of mass society. Its proposed alternative is personal autonomy, individualism and cultural sophistication. The *conservative critique* took issue with pauperisation and the corrosive effect of modernisation on the moral fabric of society. Instead, it held up the ideal of universal human dignity, the mutual dependency of social classes and the moral responsibility of the powerful.[4]

The social and artistic critiques were not restricted to the personal, but became drivers of social change in collective formations.[5] Their ideas about a different, better world represented a source of inspiration and renewal in the economic sphere, and their criticisms have been integrated into the practices of capitalist institutions in an ongoing, system-stabilising process. The labour movement's social critique formed the starting point for a 'democratic capitalism'[6] with employment rights, social security, and health and safety laws, and warded off the threat of real social and economic revolution. The artistic critique that emerged in the 1970s was also successively co-opted by various institutions.[7] Capitalism responded by expanding the supply of individualised goods ostensibly conveying cultural distinction. The 'job for life', which had formed the institutional basis for a broadly uniform lifestyle, has been superseded by a never-ending succession of personal trials and professional tribulations.

Incorporating the praise and criticism – 'recuperating' its creative energy[8] – would, it was argued, initiate innovation by un-leashing individual creativity and expanding personal responsibility. The interaction between artistic critique and capitalist institutions created a 'new spirit of capitalism', that served to legitimise the emerging forms of socio-economic organisation.[9] Capitalism once again turned out to be a highly responsive system. The cycles of recuperation sparked by the social and artistic critiques also had certain real liberalising and democratising effects, strengthening social rights and individual liberties.[10]

The ecological critique is a child of the twentieth century. It argues that our current society is 'destroying civilisation' and fundamentally rejects the ideas of progress championed by the social and artistic critiques. Unlike its predecessors, the ecological critique 'appears to have no preference for any particular political model'.[11] Its ideological spectrum runs from economic democratisation to authoritarian transformation. It is, as Chiapello argues, by no means inevitable that the ecological critique will be as amenable to liberalisation as its social and aesthetic predecessors. As such, the ideas and practices of the new climate movement look like an attempt to walk a very narrow line between democratisation and de-democratisation.

Another salient structural difference can be identified here. While the social and artistic critiques emerged out of concrete contemporaneous *experiences* (specifically capitalist exploitation and social repression) the ecological critique is principally *expectation-based* and essentially directed towards preserving the status quo. Of course certain manifestations of the climate crisis can already be observed: wildfires, drought, a slight rise in sea levels. But these are trivial in comparison to the magnitude of expected disaster that motivates the new climate movement.

If we are seeking a sociological understanding of the ecological critique and its ideas about the kind of life required by an adaptive society, it is not enough just to speculate. We need to seek empirical pointers. I would suggest that examining real-life practices of adaptation can generate empirically founded hypotheses about the central ideas associated with a radically adaptive way of life. And that brings us straight to the question of where experiences of this kind might be found today, experiences that lend us insights into adaptive mobilisation and the complex practices of survival.

The pandemic as adaptation

We have recent and very concrete experience with a survival-threatening crisis and the associated adaptive (de-)mobilisation. In early 2020, Western societies began to realise that Covid-19 – unlike SARS (2002/2003) or the multiple Ebola outbreaks in West and Central Africa since 2014 – was going to be a global pandemic. This set off a cascade of practices that touched on the two central axes of social adaptation: the hierarchy of cultural values and the perceived legitimacy of societal responses.

When China locked down the city of Wuhan, confining millions of residents to their homes, citizens of the liberal Western democracies reacted with horror. They could not imagine agreeing to such restrictions on their freedom, rigidly enforced without democratic process. Some had more cynical thoughts. Would capitalist societies really place more value on the lives of comparably few (mostly older or sick) people than on keeping the economy running?[12] Did the capitalist state not derive its legitimacy primarily from its function of guaranteeing economic growth? Had decades of neoliberal restructuring not infiltrated that mantra into every last pore of society, into its subjective value system? Whether one identifies bourgeois liberty or the capitalist profit drive as the ultimate value, the first lockdown in March 2020 suspended both for the sake of an initially unconditional orientation on protecting human life.

Under the pressure of acute crisis, instruments that had previously been regarded as beyond the pale were suddenly deemed opportune. Rules were changed at the drop of a hat, public spending was unleashed on a huge scale, employers' rights were curtailed by rules requiring their staff to work from home,[13] and restrictions were placed on the number of people permitted in shops and offices at any one time. This was essentially a gigantic experiment in adaptive reorientation. National borders, which the privileged citizens of the Global North had become accustomed to passing through with ease, were suddenly closed in an abrupt reversal of globalisation.[14] European states and companies raced to develop digital systems for contact tracing, and the great controversy over digital surveillance was forgotten in an instant. These collective adjustments created huge challenges at the personal level. When the requirement to attend school was suspended, parents were forced to choose between exposing their child to the risk of attendance or pausing their education. Students were kept out of their universities for months. Residents of care homes were prevented from leaving, their friends and relatives forbidden to visit. In other words, all instances of social contact were subjugated to society's new rules, in a context in which it became impossible to distinguish between individual and collective adaptation.

We can conceptualise the pandemic as a dress rehearsal for future crises. It can tell us a great deal about how contemporary societies respond to disaster,[15] and was itself a concrete expression of the social consequences of the environmental emergency.[16] As an incident of global self-harm[17] that focussed absolute attention on survival, it exhibited a number of structural similarities to crises driven by climate change. The origins of both the Covid virus and climate change lie within human society. While both could theoretically have been prevented, it is now too late for that. Now there is no alternative to adaptation.

It is no coincidence that social infrastructures became the epicentre of adaptation.[18] Infrastructures ensure the operation of basic societal functions. Transport and communications networks enable the flow of goods and information, public services provide socialisation and education, while the health service saves lives and treats the sick. This is a *critical* sphere for the reproduction of society. These are processes without which society simply cannot function in the longer term, because they are *critical* for its continuing existence. The existence of society is intimately bound up with its infrastructures.[19] Infrastructures are products of societal coordination and expressions of normative priorities. This makes them decisive for absorbing and adapting to the effects of crisis.[20] For example, the availability of digital communication was a crucial precondition for adapting the organisation of labour; the availability of intensive care beds and the roll-out of vaccination infrastructure defined the material possibilities of healthcare responses. So infrastructures define the possibilities and limits of collective adaptation. In the event of crisis, they need to be both robust and flexible. And it is in crisis that they demand the most of their staff, whose contributions form the basis of *societal* adaptation.

It is no coincidence that new social categories emerged to ac-knowledge the essential nature of certain activities. Social rights and obligations were reconfigured in accordance with their relevance to reproduction (in other words survival). If we are interested in exam-ining adaptation as a question of experience rather than expectation, we are inevitably drawn to the question of the normative positioning of those working in the relevant critical infrastructures. Moreover, their experiences – and criticisms – of adaptation in response to cri-sis point to ideas about a better society and a better way of life that could emerge from successful handling of survival threats.

The quotes cited in the following originate from a set of inter-views conducted at the height of the pandemic.[21] The subjects were key workers, whom we asked about their experiences under those exceptional circumstances and their thoughts about society. My interpretations of the empirical material are inevitably explorative, and any generalisations are therefore tentative in nature. I begin by reviewing the structural conditions that characterise the field, followed by an overview of the topics most commonly raised in the interviews (enormous pressure of work, social division, sense of purpose). Positivity about the work is almost always associated with positive experiences of cooperation. I then sketch out a typology of the social criticisms mentioned in the interviews, identifying three main points: a culture that rewards narcissism, an exclusively profit-driven economy, and a state weakened to the point of incapacity. In their place, the interviewees express a desire for greater socio-economic equality, functioning hierarchies and a protective iteration of vertical authority. Those are the pillars of their 'good society'. Finally, I turn to the political perspectives implicit in these criticisms and visions, which exhibit interesting parallels to the ecological critique articulated by the new climate movement.

We are dealing with areas defined as 'critical infrastructure', which is defined in German law as 'ensuring the provision of important and essential goods and services'.[22] These include 'in particular the healthcare sector, utilities and food supply, public administration, transport and IT infrastructure, social work and education, cleaning, hygiene and waste disposal, firefighting ... and law and order'.[23] As surveys show, those who work in these areas tend to have low occupational prestige, in no small part on account of their comparatively low pay and other disadvantages.[24] These are often traditionally female-dominated occupations (although not exclusively: the police service skews heavily male) and have always been subject to pressure to cut costs and increase productivity.[25] There is a fair degree of social heterogeneity, however: the term 'health worker' covers everything from hospital cleaner to surgeon.[26]

While these occupations have always been characterised by structural stress and overwork, the pandemic turned the dial up to eleven (and beyond), especially in the areas worst affected, such as the health service, social care and policing. Staff complained of immense overwork and utter exhaustion, especially at the height of the pandemic. Speaking in the summer of 2021, one nurse described the state of emotional collapse she had experienced the previous spring: 'We worked to the point of exhaustion, and we really did go to work every single day, and sometimes I cried before going to work during the pandemic, because I was just at the end of my tether.'

These kinds of experiences were frequently described as a simple worsening of stresses that were in fact already prevalent throughout the health and care systems and the police, stemming in particular from chronic underfunding and understaffing. As one male nurse noted:

Most of the nurses at our hospital are very overworked, absolutely.
We're noticing it now, it got worse after Covid. [...] Sometimes
colleagues have to work seven, eight, nine days in a row. And at
some point, they're just done, aren't they. Especially if they're on
nights or have a string of early shifts. [...] People often say that
there should be more support for nurses, but they haven't had any
real support. The hospitals got help but the nurses didn't.

His experiences working in a hospital reflect the social conditions
more generally, which he experienced as divided and inequitable:

Well the big companies like Amazon certainly made enormous
profits and came out winners. The pharmacies did very well for
themselves too. Many hospitals were just fine. [...] And the losers
were the small businesses and people doing casual and part-time
work. [...] The big firms like Lufthansa, like BMW, well they're very
powerful aren't they, and the government just does what they tell
it to. I don't think there are really very many politicians who still
serve the people.

Many of the interviewed essential workers attributed their structural
overwork and stress to a *divided social order* in which the interests
of people like them are not politically represented. Those who were
lower in the workplace hierarchy were most likely to feel powerless.
Whether they were talking about their work, social inequality,
economics or politics, they described a society divided between the
powerful and the powerless, the elites and the ordinary people. This
was rarely associated with a fundamental rejection of hierarchies.
Instead, there was a broad acknowledgement of the fundamental
functionality of hierarchies, with which they were familiar from
their work. But they did articulate a specific *lack of contact* with, even
alienation from the upper reaches of the hierarchy, both at work and
in society at large. The head of a psychiatric ward, for example, noted
specific problems in social infrastructure, but also acknowledged
the massive burden on the population at large, with whom she felt
she shared the same boat. She located the reasons for this – quite
typically for our sample of essential workers – in the remoteness of
the ruling elites:

Of course it was the ordinary people who paid the price again, like they always do. The essential workers. [...] And I think working from home must be a nightmare if you have kids at home. [...] The winners will be the ones who got into the surgical mask business, or, I don't know, invented some weird kind of disinfectant ... [...] They'll be laughing all the way to the bank. The workers worked twice as hard, but not the bosses. Maybe they got some kind of bonus to keep them quiet but basically, I think they got hung out to dry, like always. [...] Sometimes I just have no idea what the people in charge are up to. They certainly aren't looking out for us. It's very frustrating. [...] It's not about us citizens anymore, how to make the best of it for us, that's not how I see it. [...] None of the politicians have charisma, none of them actually care about the young people, the children, the school pupils, all the people who are poor or sick.

The pandemic was felt to have exacerbated these trends and widened the gap between ordinary people and those in charge. Few of the interviewees had thought about giving up their job. This was not because they viewed it as an inescapable duty, but because they regarded their work– despite overwork and exploitation – as a social praxis with purpose and meaning. The subjective value of their work was predicated above all on micro-milieus of solidarity and meaningful social interactions. The fact that clear, systematic instructions are vital for their own work explains the absence of a fundamental criticism of social hierarchies. For example, the phrase 'living in the moment'[27] cropped up several times in interviews with police. Normally, the police would expect to be 'ahead of events', in a position of control. Instead, during the pandemic, they shared the same focus on the present that we identified as a characteristic of adaptive praxis. If you are living 'in the moment', you are at least keeping up with events. You are experiencing agency, making a difference.

The interviewed police sometimes used the expression 'living in the moment' to describe the feeling of unity with their role, with their colleagues, and to some extent with a particular section of the population. It is certainly problematic if they feel they are losing this sense of security. For example, one interviewed policeman, who is also a local councillor for the conservative CDU, was visibly disappointed by certain experiences, which had alienated him from a milieu that he felt actually belonged on his side:

> It used to be that we mostly got aggro from the extreme left. And in the mainstream at least you could still talk with people normally. [...] And now suddenly the mainstream or the respectable right, they also tend to assume that policing will be more by force than consent [...]. It used to be that the right, the conservatives would say: 'Break that left-wing demo up, by force if need be, they're just a bunch of troublemakers.' Now it's exactly the other way round. But the police are still the enemy. That's the only thing that's stayed the same. [laughs] I think that's really stressful for a lot of colleagues. [...] They [lockdown opponents] think they have the right to demonstrate just how they want, whatever the price. And you know what's mad about that? They used to be the law-and-order fans and now they don't give a damn about law and order.

Like exploitative working conditions and the fatal impact of the profit motive in the provision of public goods, hostility from formerly supportive social milieus was regarded as unfair and disappointing. At the same time, however, these kinds of experiences also strengthened internal cohesion within these groups: the sense that one can depend absolutely on one's colleagues. The autonomy of the teams – the individuals on whose cooperation one must rely – is therefore a central source of job satisfaction. This was expressed by the head of a palliative care unit in Lower Saxony, who regarded his colleagues as 'close partners' with whom he 'shares everything', and also by a young police officer from Frankfurt am Main who stated with pride that he and his colleagues would 'die for each other'.

Internal cohesion does not necessarily require external hostility. It is sustained by the collective accomplishment of challenging tasks. Interventions in the autonomy of the groups – whether by way of their institutional funding, by superiors outside the team or through administrative rules imposed by politicians in response to the pandemic – came in for heavy criticism. The respondents exhibited great confidence in their own competence, and generally also in that of their colleagues. This confidence was acquired by those who remained and coped successfully with the structural challenges of the profession. In other words, those who demonstrated exceptional adaptation through their *essential pragmatism*.

Forceful *criticism* of existing conditions extended far beyond the interviewees' own work, although the latter was frequently the explicit starting point for critical reflections on the broader situation. Across all the investigated occupations we found three central, interconnected motifs: a *cultural critique* of a society described as egotistic or narcissistic; an *economic critique* of the profit-driven system; and a *political critique* of a weak and incompetent state.

The interviewed essential workers are social individuals who were generally very aware of their significance for the reproduction of the modern way of life and not afraid to say so. They were highly critical of the trends they observed, identifying the prevalence of egotism throughout society as a central problem. This was frequently ascribed to the economic and social elites, but also seen more generally as a drain on society. One male nurse regarded it as society's greatest bane:

> This very narcissistic way of thinking. This very narcissistic world view. They're all just putting themselves first. They all think they are the best, the strongest. There's less and less cooperation. If they can screw someone over, rob them blind, then they just do it, it just happens. [...] Like I already said today, this great divide through society is a huge issue, isn't it. All the strife and disagreement.

The *narcissism* mentioned here alludes above all to egotism and self-interest. It contrasts sharply with the feeling of powerlessness experienced by essential workers – although they also derive a sense of moral satisfaction from their sacrifices and from playing a constructive role in a functional hierarchy. They see the idealisation of radical individualism as a smokescreen for greed and manipulation. One teacher ruminated on social inequality and its power-stabilising function:

> Well you see Richard Branson flying into space or whatever be-
> cause he just doesn't know what to do with himself. Yeah, because
> he's bored or whatever, he starts a race, competing with the other
> two rich blokes. And on the other side you're sitting at home or
> whatever and you see all that and you think, brilliant, bread and
> circuses. That's supposed to keep us quiet.

A psychologist identified values as a central problem and put his finger on contradictions in personal goals:

> The money thing plays a very different role for young people than
> it does for older folks. I don't know if I'm seeing it wrong. Somehow,
> they say there are more young millionaires now than ever before or
> something. [...] So somehow they all want to be individualists, and
> somehow everyone wants to be the best, the greatest, the perfect
> one, exactly. And I think that's a really huge problem.

This striving for singularity, which she felt was encouraged by society, was less about personal autonomy than an attempt to live up to
a cultural ideal that was – for banal reasons of arithmetic – denied
to all but a few. After all, she said, they can't all be 'the best'. Society's
cultural incentives, she said, were wrongly configured. They encouraged competition and egotism, but inevitably produced subjective
disappointment.

As these quotes suggest, the social critique expressed by the
interviewees frequently hinted at an underlying *critique of capitalism*
that was often rather vague but occasionally astonishingly precise.
It also encompassed criticism of democracy, which was regarded as
a system that is incapable of taming the egotism of the elites. When
asked what lessons should be drawn from the pandemic, one junior
doctor responded without hesitation: 'That capitalism just doesn't
work!' She laughed out loud and continued:

> I think we saw that very clearly. That our school system is pretty
> unfair. That, altogether, health is not a commodity to be sold for
> profit, but something everybody should have a right to, whether
> they are rich or poor. [...] If it weren't for those capitalist mech-
> anisms, you wouldn't have all that pressure for the hospitals to

operate economically. You wouldn't have that pressure to rush pa-
tients through and send them off home as fast as possible. And
you wouldn't have all that pressure in the ordinary GPs' surgeries
either. Without the pressures of capitalism, you could make sure
that people had a pleasant working environment. You could simply say 'Well we're not going to do 120 percent now; 100 percent
will be just fine.' [...] That would be quite an improvement.

While this may sound like a radical critique of the system, it transpires on closer examination to represent above all a defence of her
own expertise, which is too important to exploit for capitalist profit.
Our interviewees rarely expressed fundamental criticism of the capitalist economic system quite so clearly and directly. But they did
generally exhibit a strong sense of fairness, with a sharp awareness
of discrimination and exploitation and the negative impact of both
on social justice and cohesion.

The cult of individualism was sometimes criticised as avar-
icious and manipulative, sometimes excused as ignorance. It was
contrasted with an ethic of the modest, honest and authentic –
contrasting the interviewees' own principles with the perceived
egotism of society. The *cultural critique* generally weighs more heavily
here than more materialist critiques of capitalism. The desire for
self-realisation is understood as an essential part of a majority
culture that is based on a false and hollow life model, which the
others have 'somehow' been unable to escape. As a policewoman
from Bavaria put it:

Somehow nobody is willing to do without or make a sacrifice.
There's your egotistical society again. Everybody wants to travel
and fly, all the time and wherever they want, to be free. Well I can
understand it too really, somehow. [...] I think there are other ways
to be happy though, but somehow a lot of people don't manage
to, they aren't able to think any differently.

The others' supposed superficiality casts the respondents' own sacrifices in a positive light, counterposing their own meaningful way of
life (characterised by frugality, solidarity and collective values) with

the shallowness of the self-seeking.[28] For instance, another police-woman related how the experiences of the pandemic had confirmed her fundamental sense that the culture industry and the obsession with personal growth were distracting attention from the truly important questions of life. Moreover, she felt that society's emphasis on cultural singularisation created 'immature' subjects who lacked basic human abilities. She felt that the reduction in cultural distractions during the pandemic had enabled people to rediscover buried or forgotten aspects of authentic meaning, which often contained a ludic element:

> For me it just confirmed that, y'know, a lot of people just stress themselves out too much, they're much too dependent on materialistic things, y'know, and so many people aren't really able to keep themselves occupied and they have become so immature. You know, the things you did as a kid, just thinking something up, something you could play, just doing it. As a child you just climbed up a tree and had fun there. I think a lot of people are lacking that. They've become dependent on things like bars, cafés, discos, and of course that's fun, isn't it, now and then, but they've become completely addicted, in my opinion. And maybe they could all learn that you can pass the time differently [...], and maybe give those basic values another chance. What is truly important?

This passage reveals a specific, modest concept of freedom, which was expressed in very similar terms by many of the essential workers: simple, unassuming, quietly confident. 'Mature' attributes that enable a person to assume responsibility for self and others. This was not merely a normative orientation, but described the central tenets of their own praxis. Here, situations of freedom were generally associated with moments of control over time and an absence of stress: as a child in a tree, looking out across your own garden, in the gym with your best friend, or interacting with your children. That's what is 'truly important'.

Such practices were not the respondents' lived reality; they possessed no realm of private happiness untouched by the problems of broader society. In fact, experiences of that type of freedom were extremely rare, especially during the pandemic. And above all, their desired way of life was threatened by social conditions in which positive experiences were overshadowed by exhaustion, exploitation and hostility. To the essential workers, the culturally dominant egotism of the majority society provided a comprehensive explanation of their own powerlessness and lack of political representation. Under this perspective, a good life is, almost by definition, only possible in conducive micro-milieus – principally work and family. Competence, authenticity and simplicity form the pillars of the adaptive life.

It is worth noting that this stance tends to uphold the conditions it criticises. Explaining one's own powerlessness as an effect of an egotism that is inherent to the culture means that it is almost impossible to imagine a society that does anything different, still less that one might be able to influence this. Instead, ideas about the future are dominated by dark visions of more of the same. A psychological counsellor said she thought that negative individualisation trends would only get worse. She associated this with the enforcement of capitalist imperatives, which she regarded as the current society's cultural base:

> I think it's just going to get worse and worse. Most of all, the capitalist thing will get worse. The egocentric, the egotistical is just getting bigger and bigger, um, and that increasingly becomes the feeling of being something special, doesn't it? 'I've got to be better', that's growing and growing. This trend for perfectionism. [...] And then nobody will be interested in anybody else. I think it's more, like, that everybody [will be] in sub-communities, but I think if you take a step back everyone will just be, like, how can I get the best possible out of myself, whatever the price? And you see that ruthlessness. How can I get one over? Who gives a shit? Um, well, this egotistical thing, it's just going to get bigger, bigger and bigger, and I don't want to say that the human race, that all the people are becoming narcissists or whatever. But [...] they must always be thinking: How can I get more and more out of myself?

The criticism of compulsive perfectionism (progress!) expressed in these passages suggests an expectation of social decline. Many of our essential workers had much more drastic expectations and fears. In their eyes, egotism would ultimately lead to the downfall of the society they work so hard to protect. In real crises, a policeman and former soldier said, highly individualised societies are incapable of organising collective forms of survival. Alluding to the supply chain disruption and temporary shortages of the pandemic, he employed the analogy of war:

> If the food supply breaks down here ... Well, if you just take a look at the reports from the Yugoslav wars and so on. How did one of them describe it? First of all, the weak died. And then the others fought over what was left. Hunger is one of the biggest motivators for us humans. And if the food supply really had broken down, [...] well, you just have to wonder whether there wouldn't have been something like civil war.

From the policeman's perspective, the only conceivable way forward is to pursue universal collective goals: 'Today, the individual is valued more highly than the community. We need to teach people that the community is more important, that it's not just the law of the jungle.'

Steering society towards objectives more important than individual freedom – as another dominant motif expressed by interviewees from various essential services – is the task of the state. But the state no longer does this. It fails to represent those who ensure that society continues to function. Instead, the state is dominated by individualistic egotism, as one nurse noted in relation to the payments pocketed by certain German politicians for their role in procuring personal protective equipment during the early phase of the pandemic:

> For example, it would've been nice if a crisis like that had taught us that there are more important things than money. But that deep urge to enrich yourself as soon as the opportunity arises, that still seems to apply. That's not the state's intention I think, it's not deliberate, but it seems that's just how people tick [...].

Apart from attributing specific problems to the personal greed of individual functionaries, the critiques of the state vary in their radicalism and are not argued exclusively in terms of cultural influences. But they do concur on one central point: the inability to generate *legitimacy* – in the sense of popular outcomes – through effective action, which the essential workers regard as the entire point of politics.[29] A psychiatric nurse in Lower Saxony spoke for many when she criticised the state's responses as too slow and inefficient – which became glaringly obvious during the pandemic:

> To my mind, the government was kind of asleep at the wheel, and then they were chopping and changing all the time. And now each federal state just does as it pleases. That's not how I'd do it. That applies to the pandemic of course, but also the schools in general. Well, it was a poor show. [...] The politicians should've done things very differently. Should've been clearer for a start and perhaps responded more quickly. And also avoiding, avoiding the fragmentation everywhere. Yeah, [the incidence rate] was a good deal higher in some regions than others, but sometimes I would have wished … because sometimes you just didn't know what's what anymore. It was different everywhere. I didn't like that. I'm normally not at all the type for 'one size fits all' and [...] everyone doing the same. Not my thing at all otherwise. But I think in this case it would have been called for.

Here, the inadequacy of the state's response is attributed directly to the regional differentiation of political powers and pandemic-related measures. The decentralisation of power is rejected, its concentration supported. The possibility of holding an independent position is ignored (subpolitics!). There is absolutely no expectation of efficiency gains for the state through an expansion of democratic participation. And absolutely no element of personal political activism, nor any conspicuous desire for democratic discussion and decision-making. Instead, good – meaning centralised – government is seen as the way to master the complexity of the crisis. Having the same rules for everybody can be interpreted as a wish for greater clarity and simplicity, and also a desire for fairness in a situation where there is a strong sense of being exploited.

As practitioners of adaptation, the essential workers feel they are living *the right life under the wrong conditions*. Although they feel powerless in a dichotomous social order that reifies self-interest and individualism and is administered – for better or worse – by a disinterested state that is unwilling or unable to govern, they experience successful subjectification in their immediate social circle and their confidence in their own abilities (although these are not acknowledged politically). They tackle the problems of survival and in fact create society's spaces for self-realisation. But the social realities make a mockery of their efforts.

The rot goes much deeper than pay and conditions, even if those virtually always got first mention. Looking beyond such fundamentally resolvable problems, the respondents laid out scenarios in which society implodes after neglecting the conditions of its own reproduction (and specifically the people who deal with its daily maintenance). As the pillars of stability crumble, society struggles to adapt to crisis. It survives only by radicalising the inequalities that characterise it under normal conditions. The essential worker sees no reason to make common cause with this order, in which they feel left to fend for themselves. They counterpose the ethic of a 'right life' that tends towards specific imaginings of a 'good order'.

Our interviewees emphasised four elements that make up the *concept of a good* society. Firstly, they contrasted the existing polarisation of society with ideals of greater equality, often with notable openness to diversity. One junior doctor articulated this vision especially eloquently:

A society where people are considerate towards each other, where people are not divided into winners on one side, losers on the other. We need to find a balance with most people living at a similar – let's say – level of comfort. Not just a few living the high life and a few right at the bottom of the heap. Well, now there are *many* at the bottom of the heap, and if we put them all more in the middle, maybe a few people would have a bit less luxury then, but very many people would be better off. Then somehow altogether you know that things like gender, skin colour, where someone comes from, all that doesn't matter, simply doesn't play a role. Also sexual orientation, that's irrelevant, [...] instead you should just be treated as a human being, [...] Yes, I think that would be a good society.

This quote expresses the wish for a society with less social distance between its members. One can interpret this as a solution to the problems of alienation that are associated with power asymmetries. At the same time, hardly any of the interviewees suggested a real material equalisation. The quoted doctor expresses a desire not for a society of absolute equals, but for the elimination of disadvantage and an altogether more compact social body. In other words, positional fairness to counteract centrifugal forces.

What they do not articulate is a fundamental critique of power as the integrating force in society, and, in fact, the idea appears not to play any significant role at all. Quite the opposite. Essential workers know from experience that hierarchies of knowledge and authority are vital at all levels of society. Problems occur when those in charge exceed their powers, for example, when political/administrative rules interfere with functioning work processes. This brings us to the second element of a good society: functioning hierarchies and clear leadership to address the perceived dysfunctionalities of social coordination. As one care manager noted:

The health minister [...] is also responsible for our working conditions. But we decide how they are implemented on the ground. That's me and my colleagues. [...] [H]ow I feel at work and how we feel as a team, that's our own responsibility, not the health minister's.

While politics defines the framework, he says, it is down to the actors on the ground to deal with each concrete situation. Crises demand exceptional leadership, above all to protect those operating at the sharp end. His personal lesson from the pandemic is:

Things just run more smoothly in crises and emergencies if everyone is following a single leader. The person giving the orders might occasionally get it wrong or whatever, maybe make a mistake or something. There's no point challenging it, is there, you just have to do what the person in charge says. If everyone just does it their own way, then things get completely out of hand. That's the principle I tried to follow.

Approval of *hierarchies of knowledge and responsibility* – resulting from personal experience at work – is, as the above passages convey, directly connected with a broad acceptance of (and frequently an explicit wish for) *vertical authority* to enforce rules against the individual egotisms of the culture. This is the third central element of the good society. One interviewed childcare worker described her work as rule-oriented communication of the skills required to live in a free society. She saw great potential for aggression in members of society who fail to obey the rules. More generally – and absolutely in line with the criticism of egotism that characterises this field – she regarded rule-breaking as characteristic of the current society. She described the pandemic as a revelation. When face masks were made compulsory on public transport, she expected the rule to be widely ignored by many and was thrilled to find that the crisis had in fact motivated people to obey the rules. In her eyes, society had found its true nature in and through the pandemic. She was sceptical about the easing of restrictions, on the other hand, and would like to have seen harsher punishments for transgressions:

> I thought it wasn't good that they eased the lockdown rules again very quickly, they were very quick to do that, because I also said, if they let go now, then we'll have even higher incidence rates in one or two months at the latest. And that's exactly what happened then. And it was crap that it wasn't enforced properly. What I thought was, okay, if someone really flaunts the rules, for example, if I see two teenagers meeting up, then they shouldn't just get a warning. If you ask me, they should each be fined two hundred euros. That kind of thing is just anti-social and egotistic.

This wish for rigorous vertical authority to counter the egotism of the individual was widespread, and addressed in particular to the state. The government's impotence was noted with incredulity. One policeman said it seemed to him that the state was failing to do its duty:

> The point of politics and politicians is to change things. That's what they're elected to do, that's what they're paid to do. That's their goddamn job, so that ordinary people don't have to do it, because we have other fish to fry. That's their job. And they're paid very very well to do it.

Where state paralysis was discussed in more complex terms, the accounts often drifted (consciously or unconsciously) from complaints about the state to a relatively fundamental *critique of democracy* itself. One young policewoman for example saw the short-termism promoted by comparatively short electoral terms as a central problem. She argued that making parliament a little less answerable to the electorate would be 'progressive':

> Oh God, now we're getting really progressive aren't we. My feeling is that we need longer between elections, because I just don't think it's attractive to do climate policy, because it won't have any visible effects within the next few years, before the next elections come round. Instead you just spend and spend and maybe there's no visible result, or not one that Joe Public can see. So I think you could make things work better if you had more time to implement them.

Two things are apparent in this quote. Firstly, the desired society, which is socio-structurally compact, functionally hierarchical and vertically governed, grants its members – and this is the fourth element of the good society – more time. This not only allows a more playful relationship with the world (like the policewoman quoted on page 79). It is also a precondition for restoring rational decision-making. In the quote here, it is the political decision-makers who would benefit from greater temporal autonomy. If they felt less pressure to justify themselves to the electorate, they would be able to make necessary but unpopular decisions. Creative adaptation requires time and is not amenable to demands for rapid results. Here, the respondent's own working and living situation is reflected very clearly in her perception of political paralysis. Interviewees also wanted more time to do things *properly* in the context of a less exhausting life. They yearned to relax.

All in all, the respondents' ideas can be interpreted as reactions to stress and overwork. Reducing social distance in a more compact society would prevent exploitation by remote elites; knowledge-based hierarchisation would allow necessary and meaningful tasks to be accomplished without interference; and the enforcement of vertical authority would create stability. The potential gain for such a society is free time.

The above quote also points to specific ideas about 'progressive' politics. Many of the narratives related by essential workers were characterised by a certain creativity, which in some cases verged on naivety, but also exhibited an interestingly ludic or experimental perspective on the political sphere. The young policewoman wanted to reduce the pressure on democratic representatives by extending the legislative cycle. Another colleague pointed to the deficits of democratic representation – which gelled with his dichotomous perception of society – and the associated alienation of the political elites from the people they govern:

> Recently I took a look at the composition of the Bundestag. There was this comparison, I think it was between 2019 and sometime in the 1960s. Back then there were bakers and bricklayers in the Bundestag. Well I can see that would be tricky today. But I can understand why the idea's been raised, because it implies that the people up there are so far removed that they don't understand our problems at all. But if you reflect on things and, politically, just avoid putting your foot in it so often, […] then you can restore a closer connection. You know, a representative of the people can only represent the people if he meets them occasionally.

He identifies a representation deficit, but is not interested in rectifying it. Given the complexity of modern government, he believes that having bakers and bricklayers in parliament would be 'tricky'. He feels competent in his own field – as the baker and the bricklayer do in theirs – but does not see himself or others like him stepping into the shoes of the corrupt elites. Instead, he would like – as he states elsewhere – to see a more effective form of politics in which politicians maintain closer contact with their electorate.

This idea of liberating politics from the need to justify every decision while keeping it responsive to the people's legitimate concerns (and even tolerating irrational contradiction) cropped up repeatedly in the interviews. One childcare worker suggested internships for politicians, who she thought would make better laws if they acquired hands-on experience in relevant fields. She saw herself – in common with most of the interviewees – as a person with strong expertise in her own field, and could imagine advising decision-makers. That kind of collaboration, she believed, could produce the kind of sensible rules she would like to see introduced and enforced. One interviewed psychologist also felt that the pandemic had shown the need for rule by experts and speculated about legislation to realise this:

> At the beginning of the pandemic it seemed like they weren't lis-
> tening to the people who knew best about that kind of thing, I
> mean the virologists. They didn't listen to the experts who know
> all about stuff like that, they weren't relying on the experts. My
> sense is that they were only brought in at quite a late stage, [...]
> and I have sometimes wondered how it would be if there were a
> few rules that set it all down legally. But even then, I think there
> would still be these protests and everything, like if you banned
> prostitution for example.

She was well aware of the democratic costs of effective, evidence-based government. Protests would be inevitable because rational decisions – including in her eyes a ban on sex work – would still be contested.

Democratisation in the sense of expanding deliberative participation or subpolitical activism is not where this group is looking. Expertise and agency lie at the heart of their ideas for restructuring politics. The complexity of the political system is regarded as a problem, as exemplified by the statements of the teacher quoted below. He points to the influence of economic interests, and above all the division of powers and the need for political compromises. His perspective on the division of powers is tangibly affected by his experience of the pandemic when the courts, he argued, obstructed necessary action:

> Well even the people who make the laws can't just do as they please. You can really see how the government is under so many different influences. They aren't just under the influence of lobbyists or whatever, but also the courts and so on, which then overturn the new laws or whatever. It all has to be one hundred percent watertight if anything is going to get through and make a difference, because too many compromises have to be made. [...] And then there's Europe on top of all that, which doesn't make any of this any easier, then you know it all has to comply with European law and then in Europe, yeah, there's also some people in power, aren't there, where you think it would be better if they weren't.

Seen in isolation, the quotes presented in this chapter merely illustrate individual personal positions. Taken together, they illuminate central aspects that are characteristic of the sample. To float a tentative generalisation, the typical wishes and criticisms expressed by essential workers adapting to crisis ultimately converge (like parts of the ecological critique) in technocratic perspectives. They would like to see the alienation that typifies their situation, the narcissistic culture that exhausts them, and the associated crisis of political agency tackled through state action based on real expertise (unhampered by deliberative or representational processes) and enforced through rational rules and sanctions. The attraction of the technocratic constellation is based not primarily on expectations of future crisis (as is typical of the ecological critique) but on very concrete experiences in the here and now. Nevertheless, here too, depoliticisation rather than democratisation is the ultimate destination.

The *adaptive critique* among essential workers is characterised by a ludic/experimental element with which many of them are familiar from their work. The reproduction and survival of society, which they secure through hierarchically structured cooperation, depends systematically on elastic and proactive agency. Adaptation shapes the everyday experience of crisis and offers its own perspective of freedom, which promises concrete relief, the ascendency of competence and ultimately the emergence of a new civilisation. The policeman who dreams of a good society while expecting civil war put his finger on the utopian heart of this idea: a flourishing civilisation based on reason, free of social conflict. His ideal society would be 'Star Trek–style communism, where everybody just works for the benefit of society' and all the basic problems are solved by technology. That wish points to a practice in which the depoliticisation of survival opens up spaces for ludic experimentation. It is the wish to live the right life under the right conditions.

6. Protective technocracy

> Political life would be purified.
> *Joseph Schumpeter (1943)*[1]

As it turns out, the political essence of the adaptive society is the depoliticisation of survival. This is articulated – explicitly or implicitly – in a desire for technocracy, whether in the form of government by experts or the technical automation of central political processes.[2] Alongside personal experience and collective imagination, the process is driven by historical disappointment with subpolitical approaches and a growing awareness of the limitations of democratisation for tackling existential problems.

Criticism of democracy is nothing new, of course. It has always been an important strand of Western political discourse, especially when expressed in the guise of doubts over the competence of politicians. In fact, uncritical excitement about 'democracy' tends to be a more recent phenomenon.[3] The idea that successful democratic practice requires limits to political participation has always been part of the discussion – frequently in the sense of restricting the participation of supposedly unworthy sections of the population.

Like certain classical philosophers,[4] some of the founders of sociology were less than entirely enthusiastic about democratisation, in the sense of expanding deliberative and participatory processes. Max Weber supported Germany's democratisation after the First World War, but what he had in mind was something like a 'plebiscitary leadership democracy'[5] – which was more about 'rigorous selection of the best political leaders than fulfilling ideals of liberty, equality and self-determination'.[6] Joseph Schumpeter was also sanguine about democracy and sceptical about its expansion.

In fact, he proposed restricting the sphere of deliberative decision-making and regarded the 'democratic method' above all as a specific form of 'competition for political leadership'.[7]

This critique was directed above all against an overly idealistic understanding of deliberative and participatory formats, and fostered a strategic depoliticisation of particular areas and questions. As far as Schumpeter was concerned, this was simply a necessary condition for the functioning of a political system whose leaders were inevitably always preparing for the next election.[8] Someone had to do the actual work of the state. But this could not be expected of the politicians, who always had one eye on public opinion and their prospects of re-election. As far as Schumpeter was concerned, a lack of democratic legitimation across broad areas of public affairs was in fact an essential precondition for a functioning democracy. Judges, central banks, state-funded universities and public bureaucracies all required a significant degree of independence. For good reason, these were spheres where experts held sway. Securing their engagement by excluding them from the 'democratic method' was essential to democratic statehood.[9]

When it comes to adaptation, however, there is no need to throw the democratic baby out with the bathwater. Instead, it is only logical if the coming adaptive society takes a fundamentally agnostic position on questions of democracy in its political system. The absolute priority is for questions of survival to be tackled at all. How that occurs is secondary. Indeed, one could argue that the demand to depoliticise the existential is nothing other than what liberal theories of the state have always regarded as the precondition for the modern social contract and thus for democracy itself: that survival must be assured before there can be any democracy at all.

The problem in late modernity is one of legitimising political rule in a situation where the threats to survival appear permanent and proliferating. That breaks with the logic of modernity, and poses the question of the characteristics of the social contract in the kind of adaptive constellation we have explored in the preceding chapters. Technocratic depoliticisation of survival is plainly a decisive element of processes of legitimacy management that might presage a 'change of form' but do not necessarily call democracy itself into question.[10]

Moreover, the adaptive critique does not require a technocracy defined by supposedly unavoidable economic and systemic compulsions (as described in the analysis of neoliberal adaptation rhetoric in Chapter 2). Instead, it demands the capacity to tackle the perceived existential problems adaptively, treating the system as an analogy of the lifeworld: our own adaptive ways of life become the model for a transformation of the political system.[11] Ultimately, these ideas boil down to a *protective technocracy* that frames and stabilises the ludic experimentation of the adaptive life and opens up spaces for meaningful cooperation.

Protective technocracy forms a significant vector of political imagination in the adaptive society. Once sensitised to the possibility, people recognise the obvious usefulness of formats of power based on technology and expertise for societies that seek stability rather than dynamism. Digital technologies play a central role in these visions. Their potential to detect, assess and respond to complex dangers ultimately raises the prospect of new forms of governance.

Popular culture supplies pointers to the potency of technocratic remedies in the self-imaginings of the coming society. The legendary computer game *Civilization*, which came out in 1991, offers a good example. The latest version – *Eras and Allies* – introduced new forms of government that become available to the players as soon as a society is globally integrated and digitally connected. While earlier versions of the game followed a relatively clear and recognisable historical path (complete with ancient, medieval, democratic, communist and fascist forms of government), now, one could say, they have added the political formations of late modernity. The latest version features an extreme neoliberal 'corporate libertarianism', a digital democracy using social media to maximise participation, and a 'synthetic technocracy'.[12] The latter is ultra-rational, data-driven and resistant to co-optation by particular interests. It strives to reflect the objective interests of the majority while ensuring that minorities are not left by the wayside. It relies on the involvement of non-human agents, in particular artificial intelligence. Algorithms initially assist human decision-makers (who are ideally experts in their field) and replace them in the longer term. Because the synthetic technocracy essentially functions as a digital super-intelligence, it has no need for democratic debate. Its attraction is the depoliticised management of social reproduction (even if bugs do still cause accidents and other inconveniences).[13]

In that respect, the synthetic technocracy aligns with a broader contemporary mood. An emerging strand of left-leaning sociology also views digital technologies as decisive tools for managing the coming society, for example in the context of a renaissance of cybernetics. The background to this is a debate about the possibilities of socialist economic planning initiated in 1920 by Ludwig von Mises:[14] The question was whether a socialist economy could be managed rationally to maximise efficiency and prosperity. Liberal economists like von Mises, and later August von Hayek, Wilhelm Röpke and Lionel Robbins, objected that socialist economic planning lacked any equivalent of the price mechanism and was therefore unable to base its calculations on reliable information. The absence of real-time data on consumer behaviour, they argued, made it impossible to calculate production capacity meaningfully or deploy resources rationally – and that left central planning without the means to keep up with rapid changes in the markets.[15]

Recent contributions have revisited that controversy, arguing that the information problem is now eminently solvable using digital technologies (whether within or outside of capitalism). Digital infrastructures for quantifying market processes in real time enable technological planning (for example through 'red' digital platforms[16]) and *adaptation* of economic processes.[17] The index fossil of this line of thinking is Project Cybersyn,[18] designed by the cyberneticist Stafford Beer for the Chilean government in the early 1970s. As Jasper Bernes puts it in his review of contemporary left-wing interest in cybernetics, Cybersyn was 'more a rhetorical than a practical success', but still offers 'a vision of a counterfactual history, in which egalitarian, computer-planned economies displaced the market'.[19]

The idea of cybernetic 'feedback infrastructure'[20] is in fact highly salient today: changes in consumer markets are instantly reported to the relevant system controllers, which adjust the respective supply structures. In the opposite direction, feedback from resource extraction and industrial manufacturing can be used to send signals to the consumer markets, for instance to offload overcapacity or manage expectations. Proponents of cybernetic economic planning point out that the most powerful corporations already employ comprehensive digital planning systems.[21] Retail giants like Amazon and Walmart use highly sophisticated digital systems to predict consumer behaviour and demand and adjust their ordering and production accordingly. The same can be said of major manufacturers.

The advocates of cybernetic counter-models propose using these feedback infrastructures to establish an economy free of the compulsions of profit and growth. Such analyses contain an echo of Schumpeter, who believed he had identified a stable, ultimately post-capitalist economy *within capitalism*.[22] Writing in the first half of the twentieth century, Schumpeter argued that dispassionate planners – rather than dynamic entrepreneurs – characterised the capitalism of his age, keeping the system stable with their technological planning tools. Where Schumpeter mourned the death of the entrepreneur, contemporary critical cyberneticists see an opportunity to realise sophisticated planning using the advanced technologies of the present age. At the heart of this concept is the idea of stabilising a system – here an *economic* system – through *adaptive transformation*.

While the cybernetic discussions outlined above revolve around solving problems within capitalism through adaptive digital technologies, the same mechanisms are also discussed in the context of the primarily ecological questions of planetary survival. In response to accelerating climate change, James Lovelock foresees a digital 'hyperintelligence' stabilising global systems and resolving the existential threats generated by modern civilisation.[23] The political trajectory here is neither subpolitical renewal[24] nor a 'democratisation of democracy',[25] neither a new liberalism[26] nor a return to plebeian democracy.[27] Nor are we looking at a revolutionary mobilisation of all forces to fight an ecological war.[28] The hope associated with adaptive stabilisation is ultimately depoliticisation: that a largely autonomous digital technology dedicated to survival will obviate the need for political conflict because the issues have already been competently resolved.

The experience of the pandemic boosted this line of political thinking. Benjamin Bratton, for example, argues for climate change to be tackled by means of a 'positive biopolitics', rudiments of which were already observed in the global responses to Covid-19.[29] The pandemic, Bratton writes, brought the collectivisation of existential threats to the forefront of public consciousness, highlighting the need for a global system of risk management. On the one hand, he argues, the virus swept away the illusion of the isolated, autonomous individual (in other words, the modern understanding of freedom). We all breathe the same air, and an understanding of our connectedness was vital to fighting the pandemic, for example through masking up. On the other hand, survival required a positive biopolitics to guide collective adaptation to the virus. Ideally, he argues, this 'epidemiological view of society' should be based on a sophisticated 'sensing layer' that would pool data from all sources: in the case of the pandemic, everything from personal test results and mobility data to hospital capacity and global weather data.[30] Such data could be fed into cybernetic simulations.

Managing human society as a whole would naturally be many orders of magnitude more complex than the Covid experience. It would, Bratton argues, require a kind of 'collective immune system'[31] on a planetary scale, capable of coordinating global responses to climate change. He calls for a planetary cybernetic control structure based on digital systems and biotechnology, which is able to translate simulation-based knowledge into appropriate social policy: 'Climate science has all of these [epistemological and technological infrastructures] except the all-important recursive enforcement part. As of yet, it cannot act back upon the climate that it represents, but it must. Just as a medical model does, it must not only diagnose but also cure.'[32] The stabilisation – or adaptation – of human society and global ecology enforced by such a technological Leviathan will be unimpeded by moral deliberations and political institutions: 'Perhaps most importantly, its functioning would not be dependent upon the moral performance of its participants nor upon the unpredictable reasonability, superstition, competence or ignorance of whoever occupies a particular formal government.'[33] Unlike Lovelock's abstract, autonomous hyperintelligence, Bratton's model is not about a passive population living happily beneath the shield of a planetary artificial intelligence. What Bratton proposes is a *participatory technocracy* in which – as the analogy of the pandemic underlines – human contributions at all levels are central to a planetary sensing system whose stabilising effect depends on recursive feedback loops. Depoliticising the existential in this way would create favourable conditions for efforts to stabilise society.

Ultimately, the visions of a protective technocracy involve abolishing the distinction between politics and science in the interests of social stability. This immediately raises questions concerning the legitimacy of such a constellation – questions that were also prominent in sociological discussions of older versions of technocratic thinking. Those earlier debates assumed a systematic difference between the spheres of politics and science, largely on the basis of Max Weber's distinction between the vocations of science and politics.[34] The duty of the scientist is to objectively rationalise modern society ('disenchantment of the world'[35]), while politics requires 'partisanship, struggle, passion'[36] (even if, as Weber famously points out, the rationalisation of society is also reflected in politics itself, for example in its bureaucratic apparatuses): 'Only someone who is sure that it will not destroy him if the world, as he sees it, is too stupid or too base for what he wants to offer it, and that he is capable of saying, in the face of all this, "nevertheless!," only such a one has the "vocation" for politics.'[37] In Weber's perspective, the decisionist principle lies at the heart of political power: 'enforcing one's own will even against resistance'.[38] On the other hand, it is also – for the same reason – precarious, its stability firmly contingent on questions of legitimacy.

That has always been central to the technocratic perspective. The sociological pioneers of technocracy like Thorstein Veblen (when the concept still meant rule by experts rather than machines) were already critical of deficits of political leadership that generated 'friction in the industrial system'.[39] The decisionist principle in politics lay at the heart of the problem of interference by laypeople in fields that actually demand expertise. If a politics beholden to capitalist interests was diametrally opposed to scientific rationality, Veblen wrote, the social system had to be revolutionised by a technically educated elite of engineers.[40] Although Veblen's technocratic vision was broadly compatible with libertarian syndicalist ideas about social organisation functioning largely without political power,[41] the autonomous organisations he inspired quickly collapsed, and the US-American technocratic movement faded away.[42]

After the Second World War, French authors like Jacques Ellul and Jean Meynauds put technocracy squarely on the agenda, discussing it as an inevitable consequence of technological development and also raising the issue of the technological management of political legitimacy.[43] This debate did not arrive in Germany until the 1960s – but was all the more vigorous when it did. The starting point was in 1961, with Helmut Schelsky's lecture on the place of humankind in the scientific civilisation.[44] The growing importance of technology, Schelsky argued, would successively diminish the importance of politics. Technical logic and constraints would supplant ideological decision-making. 'Modern technology', Schelsky wrote, therefore had 'no need for legitimacy; it "rules" because it works, for as long as it continues to function.'[45] Legitimisation becomes obsolete, he says, because scientific/technical civilisation is more about competent operation of the machinery than people ruling over people. The use of technological means to solve societal problems, he said, successively transformed democracy into a 'technical state' that needed 'no social or political revolution, no constitutional amendments, no ideological conversion'. All that was needed was the increasing use of 'scientific techniques of all kinds, and the technical state emerges within the existing structure. Yet that obscures how far we have already travelled down the road to a state where political relations among people are mediated by man-made scientific/technical factors.'[46]

Claus Offe points out a flaw in Schelsky's argument that objective necessities would make the question of legitimacy obsolete: 'The political dilemma of technocracy', he writes, consists in the fact that it must continue to motivate the population (its 'system problem') while its own inherent need for structural adjustment generates new risks that affect its legitimacy.[47] Because, he continues, the technical state rests on elements located in 'the pre-political sphere of cultural discipline and inherited subjective interests', but is always having to prioritise action in order to ensure balance,[48] the need for legitimacy actually increases under technocracy. Technocracy, as far as Offe is concerned, sets out to preserve stability but ends up generating its own forms of instability.

Behind this theory lies the assumption that technocratic government cannot supply its own legitimacy because its sole purpose is to stabilise the system (and has nothing to do with meaning or values). It lacks the cultural traditions and subjective norms that would be required to generate broad acceptance as a central source of political legitimacy. A political system

> that draws its inspiration exclusively from the sphere of technological necessity and existential imperative ... will undermine itself through the effects of political alienation: a potential for aggression whose forms, targets and class coordinates are relatively unspecific and flexible and is only rationalised as radical political criticism in a handful of socio-culturally privileged instances, is associated with a loss of control of reality and a willingness to create myths. That in turn allows the difficulty of properly grasping political processes to be irrationally bypassed.[49]

Should we take that conclusion as a warning against the kind of irrationality that proliferated during the pandemic? Or is the idea of a disempowering technocracy generating irrationality no longer relevant in the context of the adaptive society. My exploration of perspectives under the primacy of survival certainly speaks for the latter. What we are seeing is a reflexive rejection of the grammar of modernisation, an attitude to power that springs from life rather than seeking to constrain it. What people demand (or at least gladly tolerate) is certainly not the depoliticised rule of capitalist necessity, the neoliberal technocracy of financialisation and austerity. Instead, the desire for a protective technocracy is inherent to the adaptive society. It arises out of the perception of real existential issues and represents a fundamental break with the logic of capital.

If the political system is to create conducive conditions for an adaptive way of life, it will have to embrace the ludic experimentation of adaptive practice. Technocracy, as the essence of these ideas, certainly represents a plausible principle of democratic transformation because it incorporates the cultural traditions and subjective values of the adaptive society. The long-term legitimacy and stability of such a power structure would depend on how closely the existential issues driving it matched public perceptions and the extent to which such a society was capable of making participation in technocratic survival a meaningful point of reference of its ways of life. Not only is that plausible; it appears almost unavoidable in light of climate disruption, deep inequality and desperate circumstances. In that sense, protective technocracy represents the social contract of the adaptive society: the freedom of collective and individual survival supplanting the egotistic and materialistic promises of modernisation. In its positive sense, adaptation means mobilising that freedom.

Bibliography

Abbott, Andrew. 'The Problem of Excess'. *Sociological Theory* 32, no. 1 (2014): 1–26. https://doi.org/10.1177/0735275114523419 (all URLs valid as of June 2022)

Adloff, Frank, and Sighard Neckel. 'Wettlauf gegen die Zeit: Agenda für eine neue Regierung im Klimajahrzehnt'. *Blätter für deutsche und internationale Politik*, October 2021, 55–62. https://www.blaet ter.de/ausgabe/2021/oktober/wettlauf-gegen-die-zeit

Adorno, Theodor W. *Stichworte: Kritische Modelle 2*. Frankfurt am Main: Suhrkamp, 1969. English: *Critical Models: Interventions and Catchwords*, with a new introduction by Lydia Goehr. New York: Colombia University Press, 2005 [1963, 1969].

Albert, Mathias, Klaus Hurrelmann and Gudrun Quenzel. *Jugend 2010: Eine pragmatische Generation behauptet sich*. Frankfurt am Main: Fischer, 2010.

Albert, Mathias, Klaus Hurrelmann and Gudrun Quenzel. *Jugend 2015: Eine pragmatische Generation im Aufbruch*. Frankfurt am Main: Fischer, 2015.

Albert, Mathias, Klaus Hurrelmann and Gudrun Quenzel. *Jugend 2019: Eine Generation meldet sich zu Wort*. Weinheim and Basel: Beltz, 2019. https://doi.org/10.3224/diskurs.v14i4.06

Alda, Holger, Friedl Hauss, Rainer Land and Andreas Willisch. 'Erwerbsverläufe und sekundärer Integrationsmodus: Ergebnisse einer empirischen Untersuchung der Beschäftigungs-Leistung-Historik (BLH) des IAB'. *Berliner Debatte Initial* 14, no. 6 (2003): 70–85.

Almeida, Vanda. 'Income Inequality and Redistribution in the Aftermath of the 2007–2008 Crisis: The U.S. Case'. *National Tax*

Journal 73, no. 1 (2020): 77–115. https://doi.org/10.17310/ntj.2020.
1.03

Almond, Rosamunde, Monique Grooten and Tanya Petersen, eds.
Living Planet Report 2020: Bending the Curve of Biodiversity Loss.
Gland, Switzerland: WWF, 2020. https://www.wwf.org.uk/site
s/default/files/2020-09/LPR20_Full_report.pdf

August, Vincent. *Technologisches Regieren: Der Aufstieg des Netzwerk-
Denkens in der Krise der Moderne: Foucault, Luhmann und die
Kybernetik.* Bielefeld: transcript, 2021. https://doi.org/10.14361/9
783839455975

Backes, Laura, Tobias Becker, Lothar Gorris, Judith Horchert,
Anna-Lena Jaensch, Alexander Kühn, Ann-Katrin Müller, Miri-
am Olbrisch, Maximilian Popp, Marcel Rosenbach, Christoph
Scheuermann and Katja Thimm. 'Kinder der Apokalypse'. *Der
Spiegel*, 31 May 2019. https://www.spiegel.de/politik/kinder-der
-apokalypse-a-e3e8fa31-0002-0001-0000-000164181061

Baehr, Peter 'The "Iron Cage" and the "Shell as Hard as Steel": Parsons,
Weber, and the *Stahlhartes Gehäuse* Metaphor in *The Protestant
Ethic and the Spirit of Capitalism*'. *History and Theory* 40, no. 2 (2001):
153–169. https://doi.org/10.1111/0018-2656.00160

Bahl, Friederike, and Philipp Staab. 'Die Proletarisierung der Dienstleistungsarbeit: Institutionelle Selektivität, Arbeitsprozess und
Zukunftsperzeption im Segment einfacher Dienstleistungsarbeit', *Soziale Welt* 66, no. 4 (2015): 371–387. https://doi.org/10.57
71/0038-6073-2015-4-371

Barlösius, Eva. *Infrastrukturen als soziale Ordnungsdienste: Ein Beitrag
zur Gesellschaftsdiagnose.* Frankfurt am Main and New York:
Campus, 2019.

Beck, Ulrich. *Die Erfindung des Politischen: Zu einer Theorie reflexiver
Modernisierung.* Frankfurt am Main: Suhrkamp, 1993. English: *The
Reinvention of Politics: Rethinking Modernity in the Global Social Order*,
translated by Mark Ritter. Cambridge, UK, and Malden, Mass.:
Polity, 2005 [1997].

Beck, Ulrich. *Risikogesellschaft: Auf dem Weg in eine andere Moderne.*
Frankfurt am Main: Suhrkamp, 1986. English: *Risk Society:
Towards a New Modernity.* London: Sage, 1992.

Bell, Daniel. *The Coming of Post-Industrial Society*. New York: Basic Books, 1999 [1973].

Benanav, Aaron. *Automatisierung und die Zukunft der Arbeit*. Berlin: Suhrkamp, 2021.

Bendell, Jem. *Deep Adaptation: A Map for Navigating Climate Tragedy*. IFLAS Occasional Paper 2, 2018.

Bendell, Jem, and Rupert Read, eds. *Deep Adaptation*. Cambridge, UK, and Medford, Mass.: Polity, 2021.

Berkhout, Esmé, Nick Galasso, Max Lawson, Pablo Andrés Rivero Morales, Anjela Taneja, Diego Alejo Vázquez Pimentel. *The Inequality Virus: Bringing Together a World Torn Apart by Coronavirus Through a Fair, Just and Sustainable Economy*. Oxford: Oxfam International, 2021. https://doi.org/10.21201/2021.6409

Berlin, Isaiah. 'Zwei Freiheitsbegriffe'. In *Freiheit: Vier Versuche*, 197–256. Frankfurt am Main: Fischer, 2006 [1969].

Bernes, Jasper. 'Planning and Anarchy'. *South Atlantic Quarterly* 119, no. 1 (2020): 53–73. https://doi.org/10.1215/00382876-8007653

Blossfeld, Hans-Peter, and Karl Ulrich Mayer, 'Berufsstruktureller Wandel und soziale Ungleichheit: Entsteht in der Bundesrepublik ein neues Dienstleistungsproletariat?' In *Soziologische Theorie und Empirie*, edited by Jürgen Friederichs, 235–260. Opladen: Westdeutscher Verlag, 1991. https://doi.org/10.1007/978-3-322-8 0354-2_10

Blühdorn, Ingolfur. 'Demokratie der Nicht-Nachhaltigkeit: Begehung eines umweltsoziologischen Minenfeldes'. In *Nachhaltige Nicht-Nachhaltigkeit: Warum die ökologische Transformation der Gesellschaft nicht stattfindet*, edited by Ingolfur Blühdorn et al., 303–344. Bielefeld: transcript, 2020. https://doi.org/10.14361/97 83839454428

Blühdorn, Ingolfur. 'Die Gesellschaft der Nicht-Nachhaltigkeit: Skizze einer umweltsoziologischen Gegenwartsdiagnose'. In *Nachhaltige Nicht-Nachhaltigkeit: Warum die ökologische Transformation der Gesellschaft nicht stattfindet*, edited by Ingolfur Blühdorn et al., 83–160. Bielefeld: transcript, 2020. https://doi.org/10.14361/ 9783839454428

Blühdorn, Ingolfur. 'Haben wir es gewollt? Vorüberlegungen'. In *Nachhaltige Nicht-Nachhaltigkeit: Warum die ökologische Transforma-*

tion der Gesellschaft nicht stattfindet, edited by Ingolfur Blühdorn et al., 13–28. Bielefeld: transcript, 2020. https://doi.org/10.14361/97 83839454428

Blühdorn, Ingolfur. *Simulative Demokratie: Neue Politik nach der postdemokratischen Wende*. Berlin: Suhrkamp, 2013.

Blühdorn, Ingolfur, Felix Butzlaff, Michael Deflorian, Daniel Hausknost and Mirijam Mock. *Nachhaltige Nicht-Nachhaltigkeit: Warum die ökologische Transformation der Gesellschaft nicht stattfindet*. Bielefeld: transcript, 2020. https://doi.org/10.14361/9783839454428

Bohnsack, Ralf, Iris Nentwig-Gesemann and Arnd-Michael Nohl. *Die dokumentarische Methode und ihre Forschungspraxis*, Grundlagen qualitativer Sozialforschung. Wiesbaden: Springer, 2013. https://doi.org/10.1007/978-3-531-19895-8

Boltanski, Luc. *Soziologie und Sozialkritik*. Berlin: Suhrkamp, 2010.

Boltanski, Luc, and Ève Chiapello. *Der neue Geist des Kapitalismus*. Konstanz: UVK, 2013 [1999]. English: *The New Spirit of Capitalism*, trans. Gregory Elliot. London and New York: Verso, 2007.

Bonß, Wolfgang. 'Karriere und sozialwissenschaftliche Potenziale des Resilienzbegriffs'. In *Resilienz im Sozialen: Theoretische und empirische Analysen*, edited by Martin Endreß and Andrea Maurer, 15–32. Wiesbaden: Springer, 2015. https://doi.org/10.1007/978-3 -658-05999-6_2

Bourdieu, Pierre, and Jean-Claude Passeron. *Die Illusion der Chancengleichheit: Untersuchungen zur Soziologie des Bildungswesens am Beispiel Frankreichs*. Stuttgart: Klett, 1971.

Bratton, Benjamin. *Revenge of the Real: Post-Pandemic Politics*. London and Oxford: Verso, 2021.

Bricker, Jesse, Brian Bucks, Arthur Kennickell, Traci Mach and Kevin Moore. *Surveying the Aftermath of the Storm: Changes in Family Finances from 2007–2009*, Working Paper, Finance and Economics Discussion Series 2011–17. Washington, D.C.: Divisions of Research & Statistics and Monetary Affairs, Federal Reserve Board, 2011. https://doi.org/10.17016/feds.2011.17

Bröckling, Ulrich. *Das unternehmerische Selbst: Soziologie einer Subjektivierungsform*. Frankfurt am Main: Suhrkamp, 2007. English: *The Entrepreneurial Self: Fabricating a New Type of Subject*. Los Angeles et al.: Sage, 2016. https://doi.org/10.4135/9781473921283

Bröckling, Ulrich. *Gute Hirten führen sanft: Über Menschenregierungskünste*. Berlin: Suhrkamp, 2016.

Bude, Heinz. *Das Gefühl der Welt über die Macht von Stimmungen*. Munich: Hanser, 2016.

Bude, Heinz. *Deutsche Karrieren: Lebenskonstruktionen sozialer Aufsteiger aus der Flakhelfer-Generation*. Frankfurt am Main: Suhrkamp, 1987.

Bude, Heinz. *Gesellschaft der Angst*. Hamburg: Hamburger Edition, 2014.

Chandler, David, and Julian Reid. *The Neoliberal Subject: Resilience, Adaptation and Vulnerability*. Lanham: Rowman & Littlefield, 2016. https://doi.org/10.5040/9798881817329

Chiapello, Ève. 'Capitalism and Its Criticism' (2013). In *New Spirits of Capitalism*, edited by Glenn Morgan and Paul du Gay, 60–82. Oxford: Oxford University Press, 2014. https://doi.org/10.1093/a cprof:oso/9780199595341.003.0003

Dahrendorf, Ralf. *Konflikt und Freiheit: Auf dem Weg zur Dienstklassengesellschaft*. Munich: Piper, 1972.

Dahrendorf, Ralf. *Life Chances: Approaches to Social and Political Theory*. Chicago: Chicago University Press, 1980 [German 1979].

Dörre, Klaus. 'Risiko Kapitalismus'. In *Große Transformation? Zur Zukunft moderner Gesellschaften*, special issue of *Berliner Journal für Soziologie*, edited by Klaus Dörre, Hartmut Rosa et al., 3–33. Wiesbaden: Springer, 2019. https://doi.org/10.1007/978-3-658-2 5947-1_1

Dörre, Klaus, Hartmut Rosa, Karina Becker, Sophie Bose and Benjamin Seyd, eds. *Große Transformation? Zur Zukunft moderner Gesellschaften*, special issue of *Berliner Journal für Soziologie*, Wiesbaden: Springer. https://doi.org/10.1007/978-3-658-25947-1

Durkheim, Émile. *Der Selbstmord*. Frankfurt am Main: Suhrkamp, 2019 [1897].

Durkheim, Émile. *Physik der Sitten und des Rechts: Vorlesungen zur Soziologie der Moral*. Frankfurt am Main: Suhrkamp, 1991 [1890].

Durkheim, Émile. *Über soziale Arbeitsteilung: Studie über die Organisation höherer Gesellschaften*. Frankfurt am Main: Suhrkamp, 1992 [1893]. English: *The Division of Labour in Society*. New York: Free Press, 2014.

Dyer-Witheford, Nick. 'Red Plenty Platforms'. *Culture Machine* 14 (2013): 1–27.

Ehrenberg, Alain. *Das erschöpfte Selbst: Depression und Gesellschaft in der Gegenwart.* Frankfurt am Main and New York: Campus, 2004 [1998]. English: *The Weariness of the Self: Diagnosing the History of Depression in the Contemporary Age.* Montreal et al.: McGill-Queen's University Press, 2010.

Ehrenberg, Alain. 'Depression: Unbehagen in der Kultur oder neue Formen der Sozialität'. In *Kreation und Depression: Freiheit im gegenwärtigen Kapitalismus*, edited by Christoph Menke and Juliane Rebentisch, 52–62. Berlin: Kulturverlag Kadmos, 2010.

Ellul, Jacques. *The Technological Society.* London: Cape, 1965.

Emmott, Stephen. *Ten Billion.* New York: Vintage, 2013.

Endreß, Martin, and Andrea Maurer, eds. *Resilienz im Sozialen: Theoretische und empirische Analysen.* Wiesbaden: Springer, 2015. https://doi.org/10.1007/978-3-658-05999-6

Erhard, Ludwig. *Wohlstand für Alle.* Düsseldorf: Econ, 1957.

Esping-Andersen, Gøsta, ed. *Changing Classes: Stratification and Mobility in Post-Industrial Societies.* London, Newbury Park and New Delhi: Sage, 1993.

Fach, Wolfgang. 'Gouvernementalité und governance: Max Webers Herrschaftssoziologie heute'. In *Max-Weber-Handbuch: Leben – Werk – Wirkung*, edited by Hans-Peter Müller and Steffen Sigmund, 432–434. Stuttgart and Weimar: Metzler, 2020. https://doi.org/10.1007/978-3-476-05142-4_85

Felli, Romain. *The Great Adaptation: Climate, Capitalism and Catastrophe.* London and New York: Verso, 2021.

Fligstein, Neil, and Zawadi Rucks-Ahidiana. *The Rich Got Richer: The Effects of the Financial Crisis on Household Well-Being, 2007–2009*, IRLE Working Paper 121-15. Berkeley: IRLE, 2015. https://doi.org/10.1108/S0277-283320160000028011

Folke, Carl. 'Resilience: The Emergence of a Perspective for Social-Ecological Systems Analyses'. *Global Environmental Change* 16, no. 3 (2006) 253–267. https://doi.org/10.1016/j.gloenvcha.2006.04.002

Folkers, Andreas. *Das Sicherheitsdispositiv der Resilienz: Katastrophische Risiken und die Biopolitik vitaler Systeme*. Frankfurt and New York: Campus, 2018.

Food and Agriculture Organization (FAO) and United Nations Environment Program (UNEP), eds. *The State of the World's Forests 2020: Forests, Biodiversity and People*. Rome: FAO/UNEP, 2020. https://doi.org/10.4060/ca8642en

Foundational Economy Collective, ed. *Die Ökonomie des Alltagslebens: Für eine neue Infrastrukturpolitik*. Berlin: Suhrkamp, 2019. English: *Foundational Economy: The Infrastructure of Everyday Life*. Manchester, UK: Manchester University Press, 2018.

Freudenberger, Herbert J. 'Burn-Out: The Organizational Menace'. *Training and Development Journal* 31, no. 7 (1977): 26–27.

Galbraith, John Kenneth. *The Affluent Society*. Boston: Houghton Mifflin, 1958.

Geiselberger, Heinrich, ed. *Die große Regression: Eine internationale Debatte über die geistige Situation der Zeit*. Berlin: Suhrkamp, 2017.

Gerbaudo, Paolo. *The Great Recoil: Politics After Populism and Pandemic*. London and New York: Verso, 2021.

Goldthorpe, John H. 'The Service Class Revisited'. In *Social Change and the Middle Classes*, edited by Tim Butler and Mike Savage, 313–329. London: UCL Press, 1995.

Goodhart, David. *The Road to Somewhere: The Populist Revolt and the Future of Politics*. London: Hurst, 2017.

Gordon, Robert. *The Rise and Fall of American Growth: The U.S. Standard of Living since the Civil War*. Princeton and Oxford: Princeton University Press, 2016. https://doi.org/10.1515/9781400873302

Graeber, David. 'Foreword to the Routledge Classics Edition'. In Marshall Sahlins, *Stone Age Economics*, ix–xviii. London: Routledge, 2017.

Graefe, Stefanie. *Resilienz im Krisenkapitalismus: Wider das Lob der Anpassungsfähigkeit*. Bielefeld: transcript, 2019. https://doi.org/10.1515/9783839443392

Graefe, Stefanie, and Karina Becker, eds. *Mit Resilienz durch die Krise? Anmerkungen zu einem gefragten Konzept*. Munich: Oekom, 2021. https://doi.org/10.14512/9783962387525

Gurr, Ted R. *Why Men Rebel*. Princeton and Oxford: Princeton University Press, 1970.

Habermas, Jürgen. *Zur Kritik der funktionalistischen Vernunft*. Vol. 2 of *Theorie des kommunikativen Handelns*. Frankfurt am Main: Suhrkamp, 1981. English: *Lifeworld and System: A Critique of Functionalist Reason*. Vol. 2 of *The Theory of Communicative Action*, trans. Thomas McCarthy. Boston: Beacon, 1985.

Haring, Sophie. 'Herrschaft der Experten oder Herrschaft des Sachzwangs? Technokratie als politikwissenschaftliches „Problem-Ensemble"'. *Zeitschrift für Politik* 57, no. 3 (2010): 243–264. https://doi.org/10.5771/0044-3360-2010-3-243

Hillmann, Karl-Heinz, and Günter Hartfiel, *Wörterbuch der Soziologie*. Stuttgart: Kröner, 2007.

Hobbes, Thomas. *Leviathan: The Matter, Forme, and Power of a Common-Wealth Ecclesiastical and Civill*. N.p.: Floating Press, 2009 [1651].

Holling, Crawford S. 'Resilience and Stability of Ecological Systems'. *Annual Review of Ecology and Systematics* 4 (1973): 1–23. https://doi.org/10.1146/annurev.es.04.110173.000245

Horkheimer, Max, and Theodor W. Adorno. *Dialektik der Aufklärung: Philosophische Fragmente*. Frankfurt am Main: Suhrkamp, 2003 [1944]. English: *Dialectic of Enlightenment: Philosophical Fragments*. Stanford: Stanford University Press, 2002.

Hurrelmann, Klaus, and Mathias Albert. *Jugend 2002: Zwischen pragmatischem Idealismus und robustem Materialismus*. Frankfurt am Main: Fischer, 2002.

Hurrelmann, Klaus, and Mathias Albert. *Jugend 2006: Eine pragmatische Generation unter Druck*. Frankfurt am Main: Fischer, 2006.

Hurrelmann, Klaus, and Erik Albrecht. *Generation Greta: Was sie denkt, wie sie fühlt und warum das Klima erst der Anfang ist*. Weinheim and Basel: Beltz, 2020.

Infas and Institut für Wirtschaftsforschung (IFO). *Homeoffice im Verlauf der Corona-Pandemie*, Themenreport Corona Plattform, July 2021. https://www.bundeswirtschaftsministerium.de/Redaktion/DE/Downloads/I/infas-corona-datenplattform-homeoffice.pdf?__blob=publicationFile&v=4

Inglehart, Ronald. *Kultureller Umbruch: Wertwandel in der westlichen Welt*. Frankfurt am Main and New York: Campus 1995. English:

The Silent Revolution: Changing Values and Political Styles among Western Publics. Princeton: Princeton University Press, 1977.

Intergovernmental Science-Policy Platform on Biodiversity and Ecosystem Services (IPBES), ed. *Global Assessment Report on Biodiversity and Ecosystem Services of the Intergovernmental Science-Policy Platform on Biodiversity and Ecosystem Services*. Bonn: IPBES, 2019. https://doi.org/10.5281/zenodo.5657041

International Resource Panel (IRP), ed. *Assessing Global Resource Use: A Systems Approach to Resource Efficiency and Pollution Reduction*. Nairobi: UNEP, 2017. https://www.resourcepanel.org/reports/assessing-global-resource-use

International Resource Panel (IRP), ed. *Global Resources Outlook 2019: Natural Resources for the Future We Want*. Nairobi: UNEP, 2019. https://www.resourcepanel.org/reports/global-resources-outlook

Jochum, Georg, and Simon Schaupp. 'Die Steuerungswende: Zur Möglichkeit einer nachhaltigen und demokratischen Wirtschaftsplanung im digitalen Zeitalter'. In *Marx und die Roboter: Vernetzte Produktion, Künstliche Intelligenz und lebendige Arbeit*, edited by Florian Butollo and Sabine Nuss, 327–344. Berlin: Dietz, 2019.

Jugendwerk der Deutschen Shell, ed. *Jugend '81: Lebensentwürfe, Alltagskulturen, Zukunftsbilder: Studie im Auftrag des Jugendwerks der Deutschen Shell*. Opladen: Leske und Budrich, 1982.

Kaufmann, Stefan. 'Resilienz als Sicherheitsprogramm: Zum Janusgesicht eines Leitprogramms'. In *Resilienz im Sozialen: Theoretische und empirische Analysen*, edited by Martin Endreß and Andrea Maurer, 295–312. Wiesbaden: Springer, 2015. https://doi.org/10.1007/978-3-658-05999-6_12

Ketterer, Hanna, and Karina Becker, eds. *Was stimmt nicht mit der Demokratie? Eine Debatte mit Klaus Dörre, Nancy Fraser, Stephan Lessenich und Hartmut Rosa*. Berlin: Suhrkamp, 2019.

Kiely, Ray. 'From Authoritarian Liberalism to Economic Technocracy: Neoliberalism, Politics and "De-Democratization"'. *Critical Sociology* 43, no. 4–5 (2017): 725–745. https://doi.org/10.1177/0896920516668386

Koch, Claus, and Dieter Senghaas, eds. *Texte zur Technokratiediskussion*. Frankfurt am Main: Europäische Verlagsanstalt, 1970.

Kohli, Martin. 'Gesellschaftszeit und Lebenszeit: Der Lebenslauf im Strukturwandel der Moderne'. In *Die Moderne: Kontinuitäten und Zäsuren*, special issue 4 of *Soziale Welt*, 183–208. Göttingen: Otto Schwartz, 1986.

Koselleck, Reinhart, and Christian Meier. 'Fortschritt'. In *Geschichtliche Grundbegriffe*. Vol 2 of *Historisches Lexikon zur politisch-sozialen Sprache in Deutschland*, edited by Otto Brunner, Werner Conze und Reinhart Koselleck, 351–423. Stuttgart: Klett-Cotta, 1975.

Kuhn, Moritz, Moritz Schularick and Ulrike Steins. 'Research: How the Financial Crisis Drastically Increased Wealth Inequality in the U.S.'. *Harvard Business Review*, 13 September 2018.

Lange, Steffen, and Tilman Santarius. *Smarte grüne Welt? Digitalisierung zwischen Überwachung, Konsum und Nachhaltigkeit*. Munich: Oekom, 2018. https://doi.org/10.14512/9783962384449

Latour, Bruno. 'Refugium Europa'. In *Die große Regression: Eine internationale Debatte über die geistige Situation der Zeit*, edited by Heinrich Geiselberger, 135–148. Berlin: Suhrkamp, 2017. English: 'Europe as Refuge', trans. Andrew Brown, Bruno Latour's website, http://www.bruno-latour.fr/sites/default/files/downloads/P-180-REGRESSION-GBpdf.pdf

Lessenich, Stephan. 'Die Dialektik der Demokratie: Grenzziehungen und Grenzüberschreitungen im Wohlfahrtskapitalismus'. In *Was stimmt nicht mit der Demokratie? Eine Debatte mit Klaus Dörre, Nancy Fraser, Stephan Lessenich und Hartmut Rosa*, edited by Hanna Ketterer and Karina Becker, 121–138. Berlin: Suhrkamp, 2019.

Lessenich, Stephan. *Die Neuerfindung des Sozialen: Der Sozialstaat im flexiblen Kapitalismus*. Bielefeld: transcript, 2009. https://doi.org/10.1515/9783839407462

Lessenich, Stephan. *Neben uns die Sintflut: Die Externalisierungsgesellschaft und ihr Preis*. Munich: Hanser Berlin, 2016.

Lipset, Seymour M., *Political Man: The Social Bases of Politics*. Garden City, New York: Doubleday, 1960.

Lovelock, James E., with Bryan Appleyard. *Novacene: The Coming Age of Hyperintelligence*, Cambridge, Mass., and London: MIT Press, 2020.

Luhmann, Niklas. *Legitimation durch Verfahren*. Frankfurt am Main: Suhrkamp, 2001 [1969].

Luthar, Suniya S., Dante Cicchetti and Bronwyn Becker. 'The Construct of Resilience: A Critical Evaluation and Guidelines for Future Work'. *Child Development* 71, no. 3 (2000): 543–562. https://doi.org/10.1111/1467-8624.00164

Malm, Andreas. *Corona, Climate, Chronic Emergency: War Communism in the Twenty-First Century*. London and New York: Verso, 2020.

Mannheim, Karl. 'Das Problem der Generationen'. In *Wissenssoziologie: Auswahl aus dem Werk*, edited by Kurt H. Wolff, 509–565. Berlin and Neuwied: Luchterhand, 1964 [1928].

Mannheim, Karl. *Ideologie und Utopie*. Bonn: Cohen, 1930. English: *Ideology and Utopia*. Vol. 1 of *Collected Works of Karl Mannheim*. London and New York: Routledge, 1997 [1936].

Mannheim, Karl. *Konservatismus: Ein Beitrag zur Soziologie des Wissens*. Frankfurt am Main: Suhrkamp, 1984.

Mansfield, Edward D., and Nita Rudra. 'Embedded Liberalism in the Digital Era'. *International Organization* 75, no. 2 (2021): 558–585. https://doi.org/10.1017/S0020818320000569

Marcuse, Herbert. *One-Dimensional Man: Studies in the Ideology of Advanced Industrial Society*. Boston: Beacon, 1991 [1964].

Marty, Christian. 'Freiheit'. In *Max-Weber-Handbuch: Leben – Werk – Wirkung*, edited by Hans-Peter Müller and Steffen Sigmund, 70–72. Stuttgart and Weimar: Metzler, 2020. https://doi.org/10.1007/978-3-476-05142-4_12

Marty, Christian. *Max Weber: Ein Denker der Freiheit*. Weinheim and Basel: Beltz Juventa, 2019.

Marx, Karl. *The German Ideology*. New York: International Publishers, 2004 [1845/46].

Maslow, Abraham. 'A Theory of Human Motivation'. *Psychological Review* 50, no. 4 (1943): 370–396. https://doi.org/10.1037/h0054346

Mau, Steffen. *Sortiermaschinen: Die Neuerfindung der Grenze im 21. Jahrhundert*. Munich: C. H. Beck, 2021. https://doi.org/10.17104/9783406775772

Mayer-Ahuja, Nicole, and Oliver Nachtwey. *Verkannte Leistungs-träger:innen: Berichte aus der Klassengesellschaft*. Berlin: Suhrkamp, 2021.

Merton, Robert K. *On Social Structure and Science*. Chicago: University of Chicago Press, 1996.

Merton, Robert K. 'Social Structure and Anomie'. *American Sociological Review* 3, no. 5 (1938): 672–682. https://doi.org/10.2307/20846 86

Meynaud, Jean. *Technocracy*. London: Faber, 1968.

Milanović, Branko. *Die ungleiche Welt: Migration, das Eine Prozent und die Zukunft der Mittelschicht*. Berlin: Suhrkamp, 2020. English: *Global Inequality: A New Approach for the Age of Globalization*. Cambridge, Mass., and London: The Belknap Press of Harvard University Press, 2016.

Mises, Ludwig von. *Economic Calculation in the Socialist Commonwealth*. Auburn: Ludwig Von Mises Institute, Auburn University, 1990 [1920].

Morelli, Salvatore. 'Banking Crises in the US: The Response of Top Income Shares in a Historical Perspective'. *Journal of Economic Inequality* 16, no. 2 (2018): 257–294. https://doi.org/10.1007/s108 88-018-9387-9

Morozov, Evgeny. 'Digital Socialism? The Calculation Debate in the Age of Big Data'. *New Left Review*, no. 116/117 (2019): 33–67.

Müller, Hans-Peter, and Steffen Sigmund, eds. *Max-Weber-Handbuch: Leben – Werk – Wirkung*. Stuttgart and Weimar: Metzler, 2020. https://doi.org/10.1007/978-3-476-05142-4

Müller, Jan-Werner. *Was ist Populismus? Ein Essay*. Berlin: Suhrkamp, 2016.

Nachtwey, Oliver. *Die Abstiegsgesellschaft: Über das Aufbegehren in der regressiven Moderne*. Berlin: Suhrkamp, 2017. English: *Germany's Hidden Crisis: Social Decline in the Heart of Europe*, translated by Loren Balhorn and David Fernbach. London and New York: Verso, 2018.

Neckel, Sighard. 'Die Wirklichkeit des Leistungsprinzips: Ansprüche, Krisen, Kritik'. *Kurswechsel* 3, (2012): 64–70.

Neckel, Sighard. 'Im Angesicht der Katastrophe'. *Blätter für deutsche und internationale Politik*, February 2021, 51–58. https://www.blae

tter.de/ausgabe/2021/februar/imangesicht-der-katastrophe (as of March 2022)

Neckel, Sighard, and Greta Wagner, eds. *Leistung und Erschöpfung: Burnout in der Wettbewerbsgesellschaft*. Berlin: Suhrkamp, 2013.

Neubauer, Luisa-Marie, and Alexander Repenning. *Vom Ende der Klimakrise: Eine Geschichte unserer Zukunft*. Stuttgart: Tropen, 2019. English: *Beginning to End the Climate Crisis: A History of Our Future*. Waltham, Mass.: Brandeis University Press, 2023. https://doi.org/10.2307/jj.399539

Oesch, Daniel. *Redrawing the Class Map: Stratification and Institutions in Britain, Germany, Sweden and Switzerland*. New York: Palgrave Macmillan, 2006. https://doi.org/10.1057/9780230504592

Offe, Claus. 'Das politische Dilemma der Technokratie'. In *Texte zur Technokratiediskussion*, edited by Claus Koch and Dieter Senghaas, 156–171. Frankfurt am Main: Europäische Verlagsanstalt, 1970.

Parsons, Talcott. *The Structure of Social Action: A Study in Social Theory with Special Reference to a Group of Recent European Writers*. New York: Free Press, 1949.

Pelling, Mark. *Adaptation to Climate Change: From Resilience to Transformation*. London: Routledge, 2010. https://doi.org/10.4324/97802 03889046

Pfeffer, Fabian T., Sheldon Danziger and Robert F. Schoeni. 'Wealth Disparities before and after the Great Recession'. *Annals of the American Academy of Political and Social Science* 650, no. 1 (2013): 98–123. https://doi.org/10.1177/0002716213497452

Phillips, Leigh, and Michal Rozworski. *The People's Republic of Walmart: How the World's Biggest Corporations are Laying the Foundation for Socialism*. London and New York: Verso, 2019.

Polanyi, Karl. *The Great Transformation: Politische und ökonomische Ursprünge von Gesellschaften und Wirtschaftssystemen*. Frankfurt am Main: Suhrkamp, 1995. English: *The Great Transformation: The Political and Economic Origins of Our Time*. Boston: Beacon Press, 2001 [1944].

Promberger, Markus, Lars Meier, Frank Sowa and Marie Boost, 'Chancen des Resilienzbegriffes für eine soziologische Armutsforschung'. In *Resilienz im Sozialen: Theoretische und empirische Analysen*, edited by Martin Endreß and Andrea Maurer, 265–294.

Wiesbaden: Springer, 2015. https://doi.org/10.1007/978-3-658-0
5999-6_11

Reckwitz, Andreas. 'Auf dem Weg zu einer Soziologie des Verlusts'.
Soziopolis, 6 May 2021. https://www.soziopolis.de/auf-dem-weg
-zu-einer-soziologie-des-verlusts.html

Reckwitz, Andreas. *Das Ende der Illusionen: Politik, Ökonomie und
Kultur in der Spätmoderne*. Berlin: Suhrkamp, 2019. English: *The
End of Illusions: Politics, Economy, and Culture in Late Modernity*.
Cambridge, UK, and Medford, Mass.: Polity, 2021.

Reckwitz, Andreas. *Die Gesellschaft der Singularitäten: Zum Strukturwandel der Moderne*. Berlin: Suhrkamp, 2018. https://doi.org/10
.1007/978-3-658-21050-2_2. English: *The Society of Singularities*.
Cambridge, UK, and Medford, Mass.: Polity, 2020.

Reckwitz, Andreas. 'Gesellschaftstheorie als Werkzeug'. In Andreas
Reckwitz and Hartmut Rosa, *Spätmoderne in der Krise: Was leistet
die Gesellschaftstheorie?*, 23–150. Berlin: Suhrkamp, 2021. English:
'The Theory of Society as a Tool', in Andreas Reckwitz and
Hartmut Rosa, *Late Modernity in Crisis: Why We Need a Theory of
Society*, 11–94. Cambridge, UK, and Hoboken, New Jersey: Polity,
2023.

Reckwitz, Andreas. 'Lehren aus der Coronakrise: Die Politik der
Resilienz hat vier Probleme'. *Der Spiegel*, 5 March 2021. https://w
ww.spiegel.de/psychologie/corona-und-politische-resilienz-w
as-wir-aus-derkrise-lernen-sollten-a-3cea4d87-0002-0001-000
0-000176138623 (as of March 2022)

Reckwitz, Andreas, and Hartmut Rosa. *Spätmoderne in der Krise: Was
leistet die Gesellschaftstheorie?*. Berlin: Suhrkamp, 2021. English:
Late Modernity in Crisis: Why We Need a Theory of Society. Cambridge, UK, and Hoboken, New Jersey: Polity, 2023.

Redecker, Eva von. *Revolution für das Leben: Philosophie der neuen
Protestformen*. Frankfurt am Main: Fischer, 2020.

Rheingold Institut. *Psychologische Grundlagenstudie: Zum Stimmungs-
und Zukunftsbild in Deutschland: Ergebnisbericht*, Erstellt für Identity Foundation – Gemeinnützige Stiftung für Philosophie.
Cologne: Rheingold Institut, 2021.

Rifkin, Jeremy. *Die Null-Grenzkosten-Gesellschaft: Das Internet der
Dinge, kollaboratives Gemeingut und der Rückzug des Kapitalismus*.

Frankfurt am Main and New York: Campus, 2014. English: *Zero Marginal Cost Society: The Internet of Things, the Collaborative Commons, and the Eclipse of Capitalism*. New York: St Martin's Griffin, 2015.

Rosa, Hartmut. *Beschleunigung und Entfremdung: Entwurf einer kritischen Theorie spätmoderner Zeitlichkeit*. Berlin: Suhrkamp, 2013.

Rosa, Hartmut. 'Best Account: Skizze einer systematischen Theorie der modernen Gesellschaft'. In Andreas Reckwitz and Hartmut Rosa, *Spätmoderne in der Krise: Was leistet die Gesellschaftstheorie?* 151–252. Berlin: Suhrkamp, 2021. English: 'Best Account: Outlining a Systematic Theory of Modern Society', in Andreas Reckwitz and Hartmut Rosa, *Late Modernity in Crisis: Why We Need a Theory of Society*, 95–157. Cambridge, UK, and Hoboken, New Jersey: Polity, 2023.

Rosa, Hartmut. 'Resonance as a Medio-Passive, Emancipatory and Transformative Power: A Reply to My Critics'. *Journal of Chinese Sociology* 10, art. no. 16 (2023). https://doi.org/10.1186/s40711-023-00195-4

Rosa, Hartmut. *Resonanz: eine Soziologie der Weltbeziehung*. Berlin: Suhrkamp, 2019. English: *Resonance: A Sociology of Our Relationship to the World*. Cambridge, UK, and Medford, Mass.: Polity, 2019.

Rosa, Hartmut. 'Spirituelle Abhängigkeitserklärung: Die Idee des Mediopassiv als Ausgangspunkt einer radikalen Transformation'. In *Große Transformation? Zur Zukunft moderner Gesellschaften*, special issue of *Berliner Journal für Soziologie*, edited by Klaus Dörre, Hartmut Rosa et al., 35–56. Wiesbaden: Springer, 2019. https://doi.org/10.1007/978-3-658-25947-1_2

Rosa, Hartmut. *Unverfügbarkeit*. Berlin: Suhrkamp, 2020.

Rucht, Dieter. 'Jugend auf der Straße: Fridays for Future und die Generationenfrage'. *WZB-Mitteilungen* 165 (2019): 6–9.

Rucht, Dieter. *Modernisierung und neue soziale Bewegungen: Deutschland, Frankreich und USA im Vergleich*. Frankfurt am Main and New York: Campus, 1994.

Ruggie, John G. 'International Regimes, Transactions, and Change: Embedded Liberalism in the Postwar Economic Order' *International Organization* 36, no. 2 (1982): 379–415. https://doi.org/10.1017/S0020818300018993

Ruggie, John G. 'Taking Embedded Liberalism Global: The Corporate Connection'. *Taming Globalization: Frontiers of Governance*, edited by David Held and Mathias Koenig-Archibugi, 93–129. Cambridge and Medford: Polity, 2003.

Sahlins, Marshall. *Stone Age Economics*. London: Routledge Classics, 2017 [1972]. https://doi.org/10.4324/9781315184951

Sahr, Aaron. *Das Versprechen des Geldes: Eine Praxistheorie des Kredits*. Hamburg: Hamburger Edition, 2017. https://doi.org/10.38070/9 783868549072

Sahr, Aaron. *Keystroke-Kapitalismus: Ungleichheit auf Knopfdruck*. Hamburg: Hamburger Edition, 2017.

Sandel, Michael J. *Vom Ende des Gemeinwohls: Wie die Leistungsgesellschaft unsere Demokratien zerreißt*. Frankfurt am Main: Fischer, 2020.

Saros, Daniel. *Information Technology and Socialist Construction: The End of Capital and the Transition to Socialism*. London: Routledge, 2014. https://doi.org/10.4324/9781315814001

Scharpf, Fritz W. *Regieren in Europa: Effektiv und demokratisch?* Frankfurt am Main and New York: Campus, 1999.

Schelsky, Helmut. *Der Mensch in der wissenschaftlichen Zivilisation*. Cologne and Opladen: Westdeutscher Verlag, 1961. https://doi.o rg/10.1007/978-3-663-02159-9

Schrenker, Annekatrin, Claire Samtleben and Markus Schrenker. 'Applaus ist nicht genug: Gesellschaftliche Anerkennung systemrelevanter Berufe'. *Aus Politik und Zeitgeschichte* 71, no. 13–15 (2021): 12–18. https://www.bpb.de/shop/zeitschriften/apuz/im-dienst-der-gesellschaft-2021/329316/applaus-ist-nicht-genug/

Schumacher, Ernst F., *Small Is Beautiful: A Study of Economics as If People Mattered*. London: Blond & Briggs, 1973.

Schumpeter, Joseph A. *Capitalism, Socialism and Democracy*. London and New York: Routledge, 1994 [1943].

Senghaas, Dieter. 'The Technocrats: Rückblick auf die Technokratiebewegung in den USA'. In *Texte zur Technokratiediskussion*, edited by Claus Koch and Dieter Senghaas, 282–295. Frankfurt am Main: Europäische Verlagsanstalt, 1970.

Servigne, Pablo, and Raphaël Stevens. *How Everything Can Collapse: A Manual for Our Times*. Cambridge: Polity, 2020.

Silva, Patricio. 'Neoliberalism, Democratization, and the Rise of Technocrats'. In *The Changing Role of the State in Latin America*, edited by Menno Vellingo, 75–92. London: Routledge, 1998. https://doi.org/10.4324/9780429496769-4

Sommer, Moritz, Dieter Rucht, Sebastian Haunss and Sabrina Zajak. 'Fridays for Future: Profil, Entstehung und Perspektiven der Protestbewegung in Deutschland'. *Internationale Politik* 74, no. 4 (2019): 121–125. https://doi.org/10.13140/RG.2.2.32374.96327

Staab, Philipp. *Digitaler Kapitalismus: Markt und Herrschaft in der Ökonomie der Unknappheit*. Berlin: Suhrkamp, 2019. English: *Markets and Power in Digital Capitalism*, translated by Meredith Dale. Manchester: Manchester University Press, 2024. https://doi.org/10.7765/9781526172174

Staab, Philipp. *Falsche Versprechen: Wachstum im digitalen Kapitalismus*. Hamburg: Hamburger Edition, 2016.

Staab, Philipp. *Macht und Herrschaft in der Servicewelt*. Hamburg: Hamburger Edition, 2014.

Staab, Philipp, and Thorsten Thiel. 'Privatisierung ohne Privatismus: Soziale Medien im digitalen Strukturwandel der Öffentlichkeit'. In *Ein neuer Strukturwandel der Öffentlichkeit?*, edited by Martin Seeliger and Sebastian Sevignani, 277–297. Baden-Baden: Nomos, 2021. https://doi.org/10.5771/9783748912187-275

Sterk, Marjolein, Ingrid A. van de Leemput and Edwin T. H. M. Peeters. 'How to Conceptualize and Operationalize Resilience in Socio-Ecological Systems?', *Current Opinion in Environmental Sustainability* 28, (2017): 108–113. https://doi.org/10.1016/j.cosust.2017.09.003

Streeck, Wolfgang. 'Citizens as Customers: Considerations on the New Politics of Consumption'. *New Left Review*, no. 76 (2012): 27–47.

Streeck, Wolfgang. *Gekaufte Zeit: Die vertagte Krise des demokratischen Kapitalismus*. Berlin: Suhrkamp, 2013.

Streeck, Wolfgang. *How Will Capitalism End? Essays on a Failing System*. London and New York: Verso, 2016.

Streeck, Wolfgang. *Zwischen Globalismus und Demokratie: Politische Ökonomie im ausgehenden Neoliberalismus*. Berlin: Suhrkamp, 2021.

Thunman, Elin. 'Burnout als soziopathologisches Symptom der Selbstverwirklichung'. In *Leistung und Erschöpfung: Burnout in der Wettbewerbsgesellschaft*, edited by Sighard Neckel and Greta Wagner, 58–85. Berlin: Suhrkamp, 2013.

Tsing, Anna Lowenhaupt. *Der Pilz am Ende der Welt: Über das Leben in den Ruinen des Kapitalismus*. Berlin: Matthes & Seitz, 2018. English: *The Mushroom at the End of the World: On the Possibility of Life in Capitalist Ruins*. Princeton and Oxford: Princeton University Press, 2015. https://doi.org/10.1515/9781400873548

UNEP, ed. *Assessing Global Land Use: Balancing Consumption with Sustainable Supply*. Nairobi: United Nations Environment Program, 2014.

Veblen, Thorstein. *The Engineers and the Price System*. Kitchener, Ontario: Batoche Books, 2001 [1921].

Vogl, Joseph. *Das Gespenst des Kapitals*. Zürich: Diaphanes, 2011.

Vogl, Joseph. *Kapital und Ressentiment: Eine kurze Theorie der Gegenwart*. Munich: C. H. Beck, 2021. https://doi.org/10.17104/9783406769559

Wahlström, Mattias, Piotr Kocyba, Michiel De Vydt and Joost de Moor, eds. *Protest for a Future: Composition, Mobilization and Motives of the Participants in Fridays for Future Climate Protests on 15 March 2019 in 13 European Cities*. N.p.: Protest Institute, 2019. https://protestinstitut.eu/wp-content/uploads/2019/07/20190709_Protest-for-a-future_GCSDescriptive-Report.pdf (as of March 2022)

Walter, Franz. *Die neue Macht der Bürger: Was motiviert die Protestbewegungen?*, BP-Gesellschaftsstudie. Reinbek bei Hamburg: Rowohlt, 2013.

Weber, Max. *Die protestantische Ethik und der Geist des Kapitalismus*. Berlin: Holzinger, 2016 [1904/1905]. https://doi.org/10.1007/978-3-658-07432-6. English: *The Protestant Ethic and the Spirit of Capitalism*. New York and Abingdon, UK: Routledge: 2012.

Weber, Max. 'Politics as a Vocation' (1919). In *Max Weber's Complete Writings on Academic and Political Vocations*, edited and with an introduction by John Dreijmanis, translated by Gordon C. Wells. N.p.: Algora, 2008.

Weber, Max. 'Science as a Vocation' (1917/19). In *Max Weber's Complete Writings on Academic and Political Vocations*, edited and with an introduction by John Dreijmanis, translated by Gordon C. Wells. N.p.: Algora, 2008.

Weber, Max. *Wirtschaft und Gesellschaft: Grundriß der verstehenden Soziologie*. Tübingen: Mohr Siebeck, 1922. English: *Economy and Society: A New Translation*, edited and translated by Keith Tribe. Cambridge, Mass., and London: Harvard University Press, 2019. https://doi.org/10.4159/9780674240827

Winkler, Karina, Richard Fuchs, Mark Rounsevell and Martin Herold. 'Global Land Use Changes Are Four Times Greater than Previously Estimated'. *Nature Communications* 12, no. 1 (2021): 1–10. https://doi.org/10.1038/s41467-021-22702-2

Wolff, Edward N. *The Asset Price Meltdown and the Wealth of the Middle Class*, NBER Working Paper. Cambridge: National Bureau of Economic Research, 2012. https://doi.org/10.3386/w18559

Zuboff, Shoshana. *The Age of Surveillance Capitalism: The Fight for a Human Future at the New Frontier of Power*. London: Profile, 2019.

Notes

1. Introduction: Metamorphoses of adaptation

1   Ulrich Beck, *Risk Society: Towards a New Modernity* (London: Sage, 1992 [1986]), p. 28.

2   Cf. Karl Polanyi, *The Great Transformation: The Political and Economic Origins of Our Time* (Boston: Beacon Press, 2001 [1944]).

3   Cf. Klaus Dörre et al., eds, *Große Transformation? Zur Zukunft moderner Gesellschaften*, special issue of *Berliner Journal für Soziologie* (Wiesbaden: Springer, 2019).

4   Cf. Heinz Bude, *Das Gefühl der Welt: Über die Macht von Stimmungen* (Munich: Hanser, 2016).

5   Émile Durkheim, *The Division of Labour in Society* (New York: Free Press, 2014 [1893]).

6   Ralf Dahrendorf, *Life Chances: Approaches to Social and Political Theory* (Chicago: Chicago University Press, 1980 [German 1979]).

7   Cf. Andreas Reckwitz, *The Society of Singularities* (Cambridge, UK, and Medford, Mass.: Polity, 2020).

8   Andreas Reckwitz, 'The Theory of Society as a Tool', in Andreas Reckwitz and Hartmut Rosa, *Late Modernity in Crisis: Why We Need a Theory of Society*, pp. 11–94 (Cambridge, UK, and Hoboken, New Jersey: Polity, 2023).

9   For more on the pitfalls of the meritocratic principle, see Michael J. Sandel, *Vom Ende des Gemeinwohls: Wie die Leistungsgesellschaft unsere Demokratien zerreißt* (Frankfurt am Main: Fischer, 2020); Sighard Neckel, 'Die Wirklichkeit des Leistungsprinzips: Ansprüche, Krisen, Kritik', *Kurswechsel* 3 (2012), pp. 64–70; Pierre Bourdieu and Jean-Claude Passeron,

Die Illusion der Chancengleichheit: Untersuchungen zur Soziologie des Bildungswesens am Beispiel Frankreichs (Stuttgart: Klett, 1971).

10   Ronald Inglehart, *The Silent Revolution: Changing Values and Political Styles among Western Publics* (Princeton: Princeton University Press, 1977); Abraham Maslow, 'A Theory of Human Motivation', *Psychological Review* 50, no. 4 (1943), pp. 370–396.

11   Cf. Beck, *Risk Society*, op. cit.

12   Ulrich Beck, *The Reinvention of Politics: Rethinking Modernity in the Global Social Order*, trans. Mark Ritter (Cambridge, UK, and Malden, Mass.: Polity, 2005 [1997]).

13   Cf. Stephan Lessenich, *Neben uns die Sintflut: Die Externalisierungsgesellschaft und ihr Preis* (Munich: Hanser Berlin, 2016).

14   Beck, *The Reinvention of Politics*, op. cit., pp. 71–72.

15   Cf. Eva von Redecker, *Revolution für das Leben: Philosophie der neuen Protestformen* (Frankfurt am Main: Fischer, 2020), p. 183.

16   Cf. Anna Lowenhaupt Tsing, *The Mushroom at the End of the World: On the Possibility of Life in Capitalist Ruins* (Princeton and Oxford: Princeton University Press, 2015).

17   Ibid.

18   Others have developed this thought into widely circulated forecasts of the end of society as we know it. For example, collapsologists suggest that a complete failure of power systems would bring down the entire modern civilisation within just a few days, leading to 'starvation, destruction, migration, disease and war' (Jem Bendell); see, for example, Pablo Servigne and Raphaël Stevens, *How Everything Can Collapse: A Manual for Our Times* (Cambridge: Polity, 2020).

19   Cf. Klaus Dörre, 'Risiko Kapitalismus', in Dörre et al., eds, *Große Transformation?*, op. cit., pp. 3–33.

20   The Foundational Economy Collective, *Foundational Economy: The Infrastructure of Everyday Life* (Manchester, UK: Manchester University Press, 2018).

21   Cf. Max Weber, *The Protestant Ethic and the Spirit of Capitalism* (New York and Abingdon, UK: Routledge: 2012 [1904/05]).

22   To borrow from Isaiah Berlin, one could call this a negative freedom from the problematic aspects of positive freedom. Respite, rather than opportunity, is the central motif here; cf.

Isaiah Berlin, 'Zwei Freiheitsbegriffe' (1969), in *Freiheit: Vier Versuche*, pp. 197–256 (Frankfurt am Main: Fischer, 2006).

23   Cf. Hartmut Rosa, *Beschleunigung und Entfremdung: Entwurf einer kritischen Theorie spätmoderner Zeitlichkeit* (Berlin: Suhrkamp, 2013).

2. The party and the hangover: From surplus to survival

1   Bruno Latour, 'Europe as Refuge', trans. Andrew Brown, Bruno Latour's website.

2   Cf. Hartmut Rosa, *Unverfügbarkeit* (Berlin: Suhrkamp, 2020).

3   Ibid.

4   *Cambridge Dictionary*, website: https://dictionary.cambridge.or g/dictionary/english/adaptation.

5   Karl-Heinz Hillmann and Günter Hartfiel, *Wörterbuch der Soziologie* (Stuttgart: Kröner, 2007), p. 29, trans. MD.

6   Talcott Parsons, *The Structure of Social Action: A Study in Social Theory with Special Reference to a Group of Recent European Writers* (New York: The Free Press, 1949).

7   Cf. Thomas Hobbes, *Leviathan: The Matter, Forme, and Power of a Common-Wealth Ecclesiastical and Civill* (N.p.: Floating Press, 2009 [1651]).

8   Cf. Durkheim, *Über soziale Arbeitsteilung*, op. cit.

9   Cf. Émile Durkheim, *Physik der Sitten und des Rechts: Vorlesungen zur Soziologie der Moral* (Frankfurt am Main: Suhrkamp, 1991 [1890]).

10   Talcott Parsons, *The Social System* (New York: Free Press, 1979).

11   Parsons, *The Structure of Social Action*, op. cit., p. 91.

12   Cf. Émile Durkheim, *Der Selbstmord* (Frankfurt am Main: Suhrkamp, 2019 [1897]).

13   Weber's metaphor of the 'iron cage' of rationality (more recently rendered as 'shell as hard as steel') refers to the way the process of advancing rationalisation in capitalist society penetrates every aspect of life, influencing consciousness and shaping personal action. Peter Baehr, 'The "Iron Cage" and the "Shell as Hard as Steel": Parsons, Weber, and the *Stahlhartes Gehäuse*

Metaphor in *The Protestant Ethic and the Spirit of Capitalism'*, *History and Theory* 40, no. 2 (2001): 153–169; cf. *Max-Weber-Handbuch: Leben – Werk – Wirkung*, ed. Hans-Peter Müller and Steffen Sigmund (Stuttgart and Weimar: Metzler, 2020).

14   Christian Marty, 'Freiheit', in Müller and Sigmund, eds., *Max-Weber-Handbuch*, op. cit., pp. 70–72.

15   Karl Marx, *The German Ideology* (New York: International Publishers, 2004 [1845/46]), p. 53.

16   Cf.Aaron Benanav, *Automatisierung und die Zukunft der Arbeit* (Berlin: Suhrkamp, 2021).

17   Ibid.

18   Herbert Marcuse, *One-Dimensional Man: Studies in the Ideology of Advanced Industrial Society* (Boston: Beacon, 1991 [1964]), p. 75.

19   Cf. Max Horkheimer and Theodor W. Adorno, *Dialektik der Aufklärung: Philosophische Fragmente* (Frankfurt am Main: Suhrkamp, 2003 [1944]).

20   Marcuse, *One-Dimensional Man*, op. cit., p. 95.

21   Cf. Stephan Lessenich, *Die Neuerfindung des Sozialen: Der Sozialstaat im flexiblen Kapitalismus* (Bielefeld: transcript, 2009).

22   Cf. Wolfgang Streeck, 'Citizens as Customers: Considerations on the New Politics of Consumption', *New Left Review*, no. 76 (2012), pp. 27–47.

23   Cf. Philipp Staab, *Markets and Power in Digital Capitalism* (Manchester: Manchester University Press, 2024); Philipp Staab, *Falsche Versprechen: Wachstum im digitalen Kapitalismus* (Hamburg: Hamburger Edition, 2016).

24   Cf. Holger Alda et al., 'Erwerbsverläufe und sekundärer Integrationsmodus: Ergebnisse einer empirischen Untersuchung der Beschäftigungs-Leistung-Historik (BLH) des IAB', *Berliner Debatte Initial* 6 (2003); Lessenich, *Die Neuerfindung des Sozialen*, op. cit.

25   Cf. Wolfgang Streeck, *Zwischen Globalismus und Demokratie: Politische Ökonomie im ausgehenden Neoliberalismus* (Berlin: Suhrkamp, 2021).

26   Cf. Shoshana Zuboff, *The Age of Surveillance Capitalism: The Fight for a Human Future at the New Frontier of Power* (London: Profile, 2019).

27   Cf. Staab, *Markets and Power in Digital Capitalism*, op. cit.; Philipp
     Staab and Thorsten Thiel, 'Privatisierung ohne Privatismus: So-
     ziale Medien im digitalen Strukturwandel der Öffentlichkeit',
     in *Ein neuer Strukturwandel der Öffentlichkeit?*, ed. Martin Seeliger
     and Sebastian Sevignani, pp. 277–297 (Baden-Baden: Nomos,
     2021); Joseph Vogl, *Kapital und Ressentiment: Eine kurze Theorie der
     Gegenwart* (Munich: C. H. Beck, 2021).

28   Dahrendorf, *Life Chances*, op. cit.

29   Beck, *The Reinvention of Politics*, op. cit., p. 16.

30   Beck, *Risk Society*, op. cit.

31   Beck, *The Reinvention of Politics*, op. cit., p. 41.

32   Stephan Lessenich, 'Die Dialektik der Demokratie: Grenzzie-
     hungen und Grenzüberschreitungen im Wohlfahrtskapitalismus',
     in *Was stimmt nicht mit der Demokratie? Eine Debatte mit Klaus
     Dörre, Nancy Fraser, Stephan Lessenich und Hartmut Rosa*, ed.
     Hanna Ketterer and Karina Becker, pp. 121–138 (Berlin:
     Suhrkamp, 2019).

33   Ingolfur Blühdorn, 'Die Gesellschaft der Nicht-Nachhaltigkeit:
     Skizze einer umweltsoziologischen Gegenwartsdiagnose',
     in *Nachhaltige Nicht-Nachhaltigkeit: Warum die ökologische
     Transformation der Gesellschaft nicht stattfindet*, ed. Ingolfur
     Blühdorn et al., pp. 83–160 (Bielefeld: transcript 2020).

34   Ibid., p. 119.

35   Ibid., p. 124.

36   Ibid., p. 118, trans. MD.

37   Cf. Eva Wunderer, Frida Hierl and Maya Götz, 'Einfluss sozialer
     Medien auf Körperbild, Essverhalten und Essstörungen', *PiD –
     Psychotherapie im Dialog* 24 (2022), pp. 85–89.

38   Cf. Romain Felli, *The Great Adaptation: Climate, Capitalism and
     Catastrophe* (London and New York: Verso, 2021).

39   Ibid.

40   On the theoretical and practical parallels between neoliberal
     and technocratic ideas, see Ray Kiely, 'From Authoritarian
     Liberalism to Economic Technocracy: Neoliberalism, Politics
     and "De-Democratization"', *Critical Sociology* 43, no. 4–5 (2017),
     pp. 725–745; Patricio Silva, 'Neoliberalism, Democratization,
     and the Rise of Technocrats', in *The Changing Role of the State*

in Latin America, ed. Menno Velingo, pp. 75–92 (London: Routledge, 1998).

41   Cf. Blühdorn, *Simulative Demokratie*, op. cit., p. 116.

42   Ibid.

43   Felli, *The Great Adaptation*, op. cit., pp. 89–90.

44   Ibid., p. 56.

45   Paolo Gerbaudo, *The Great Recoil: Politics after Populism and Pandemic* (London and New York: Verso, 2021), p. 10.

46   Cf. Ralf Dahrendorf, *Konflikt und Freiheit: Auf dem Weg zur Dienstklassengesellschaft* (Munich: Piper, 1972).

47   Cf. Wolfgang Streeck, *Gekaufte Zeit: Die vertagte Krise des demokratischen Kapitalismus* (Berlin: Suhrkamp, 2013).

48   Ibid.

49   The financial sector's share of total profits doubled from 15 to almost 31 percent between the 1960s and the year 2000, while significant growth in corporate and state debt made it increasingly difficult to fund public services. Although the collapse of Lehman Brothers in 2008 brought that cycle to a spectacular end, capitalism's growth and stability problems remained, as did its financialised structure; cf. Staab, *Markets and Power in Digital Capitalism*, op. cit., pp. 36–37. I use the term 'real economy' to reflect the way the financial sector operates outside the rules of the rest of the economy (while still functioning as part of it via the para-economic mechanism of credit); cf. Aaron Sahr, *Das Versprechen des Geldes: Eine Praxistheorie des Kredits* (Hamburg: Hamburger Edition, 2017); Aaron Sahr, *Keystroke-Kapitalismus: Ungleichheit auf Knopfdruck* (Hamburg: Hamburger Edition, 2017).

50   Cf. Joseph Vogl, *Das Gespenst des Kapitals* (Zürich: Diaphanes, 2011).

51   Streeck, *Gekaufte Zeit*, op. cit.; Wolfgang Streeck, *How Will Capitalism End? Essays on a Failing System* (London and New York: Verso, 2016).

52   Robert Gordon, *The Rise and Fall of American Growth: The U.S. Standard of Living since the Civil War* (Princeton and Oxford: Princeton University Press, 2016).

53   For example, the entire online advertising model – which accounts for more than 89 percent of Google's profits and 98 percent of Facebook's – is based on the promise that spending in the present (on advertising) will be rewarded in the future (with sales and profits); cf. Staab, *Markets and Power in Digital Capitalism*, op. cit., pp. 12–13; Vogl, *Kapital und Ressentiment*, op. cit.

54   Cf. Neil Fligstein and Zawadi Rucks-Ahidiana, *The Rich Got Richer: The Effects of the Financial Crisis on Household Well-Being, 2007–2009*, IRLE Working Paper 121-15 (Berkeley: IRLE, 2015); Moritz Kuhn, Moritz Schularick and Ulrike Steins, 'Research: How the Financial Crisis Drastically Increased Wealth Inequality in the U.S.', *Harvard Business Review*, 13 September 2018.

55   Salvatore Morelli, 'Banking Crises in the US: The Response of Top Income Shares in a Historical Perspective', *Journal of Economic Inequality* 16, no. 2 (2018), pp. 257–294; Vanda Almeida, 'Income Inequality and Redistribution in the Aftermath of the 2007–2008 Crisis: The U.S. Case', *National Tax Journal* 73 (1) (2020), pp. 77–115.

56   Esmé Berkhout et al., *The Inequality Virus: Bringing Together a World Torn Apart by Coronavirus through a Fair, Just and Sustainable Economy* (Oxford: Oxfam International, 2021); Chuck Collins, 'U.S. Billionaire Wealth Surged by 70 Percent, or $ 2.1 Trillion, during Pandemic', Institute for Policy Studies website, 18 October 2021.

57   Branko Milanović uses the term 'hyper-wealthy' to describe individuals with net assets of at least one billion US dollars in 1987 or at least two billion in 2013. The share of global wealth owned by the richest one percent grew from 32 percent in 2000 to 46 percent in 2013. In the United States income and wealth inequality have risen to levels not seen since the early twentieth century; cf. Branko Milanović, *Die ungleiche Welt: Migration, das Eine Prozent und die Zukunft der Mittelschicht* (Berlin: Suhrkamp, 2016), pp. 52–53.

58   Cf. Daniel Bell, *The Coming of Post-Industrial Society* (New York: Basic Books, 1999 [1973]).

59   Polanyi, *The Great Transformation*, op. cit.

60   Andreas Reckwitz, *The End of Illusions: Politics, Economy, and Culture in Late Modernity* (Cambridge, UK, and Medford, Mass.: Polity, 2021).

61   Ibid., pp. 203–239.

62   Ulrich Bröckling, *The Entrepreneurial Self: Fabricating a New Type of Subject* (Los Angeles et al.: Sage, 2016).

63   Christoph Menke and Juliane Rebentisch, eds., *Kreation und Depression: Freiheit im gegenwärtigen Kapitalismus* (Berlin: Kulturverlag Kadmos, 2010), p. 7, trans. MD.

64   In contrast to Reckwitz's *Society of Singularities*, op. cit.

65   John H. Goldthorpe, 'The Service Class Revisited', in *Social Change and the Middle Classes*, ed. Tim Butler and Mike Savage, pp. 313–329 (London: UCL Press, 1995); Daniel Oesch, *Redrawing the Class Map: Stratification and Institutions in Britain, Germany, Sweden, and Switzerland* (Basingstoke and New York: Palgrave Macmillan, 2006).

66   Gøsta Esping-Andersen, ed., *Changing Classes: Stratification and Mobility in Post-Industrial Societies* (London, Newbury Park and New Delhi: Sage, 1993); Hans-Peter Blossfeld and Karl Ulrich Mayer, 'Berufsstruktureller Wandel und soziale Ungleichheit: Entsteht in der Bundesrepublik ein neues Dienstleistungsproletariat?' in *Soziologische Theorie und Empirie*, ed. Jürgen Friederichs (Opladen: Westdeutscher Verlag, 1991), pp. 235–260; Philipp Staab, *Macht und Herrschaft in der Servicewelt* (Hamburg: Hamburger Edition, 2014); Friederike Bahl and Philipp Staab, 'Die Proletarisierung der Dienstleistungsarbeit: Institutionelle Selektivität, Arbeitsprozess und Zukunftsperzeption im Segment einfacher Dienstleistungsarbeit', *Soziale Welt* 66, no. 4 (2015): 371–387.

67   David Goodhart, *The Road to Somewhere: The Populist Revolt and the Future of Politics* (London: Hurst, 2017).

68   Cf. Heinz Bude, *Gesellschaft der Angst* (Hamburg: Hamburger Edition, 2014); Steffen Mau, *Lebenschancen: Wohin driftet die Mittelschicht?* (Berlin: Suhrkamp, 2012).

69   Alain Ehrenberg, *The Weariness of the Self: Diagnosing the History of Depression in the Contemporary Age* (Montreal et al.: McGill-Queen's University Press, 2010).

70   While neuroses tend to be attributed to inner conflicts over rigid social norms, depression is seen as an expression of an individual's personal inability to fulfil social expectations; cf. Alain Ehrenberg, 'Depression: Unbehagen in der Kultur oder neue Formen der Sozialität', in *Kreation und Depression: Freiheit im gegenwärtigen Kapitalismus*, ed. Christoph Menke and Juliane Rebentisch, pp. 52–62 (Berlin: Kulturverlag Kadmos, 2010), p. 54, trans. MD (emphasis in original).

71   Cf. Elin Thunman, 'Burnout als soziopathologisches Symptom der Selbstverwirklichung', in *Leistung und Erschöpfung: Burnout in der Wettbewerbsgesellschaft*, ed. Sighard Neckel and Greta Wagner, pp. 58–85 (Berlin: Suhrkamp, 2013), p. 66.

72   Herbert J. Freudenberger, 'Burn-Out: The Organizational Menace', *Training and Development Journal* 31, no. 7 (1977), pp. 26–27; Neckel and Wagner, eds., *Leistung und Erschöpfung*, op. cit.

73   Thunman, 'Burnout als soziopathologisches Symptom', op. cit., p. 66.

74   Cf. Seymour Martin Lipset, *Political Man: The Social Bases of Politics* (Garden City, New York: Doubleday, 1960); Ted Robert Gurr, *Why Men Rebel* (Princeton and Oxford: Princeton University Press, 1970).

75   Gurr, *Why Men Rebel*, op. cit.

76   Jan-Werner Müller, *Was ist Populismus? Ein Essay* (Berlin: Suhrkamp, 2016); see also Gerbaudo, *The Great Recoil*, op. cit.

77   In other words, the countries that abandoned the statist model of economic planning after 1989. The multiple successor states to the Soviet Union and Yugoslavia are counted separately.

78   International Resource Panel (IRP), ed., *Global Resources Outlook 2019: Natural Resources for the Future We Want* (Nairobi: United Nations Environment Program, 2019), pp. 7–8.

79   IRP, ed., *Assessing Global Resource Use: A Systems Approach to Resource Efficiency and Pollution Reduction* (Nairobi: United Nations Environment Program, 2017), pp. 18–29.

80   Karina Winkler et al., 'Global Land Use Changes Are Four Times Greater than Previously Estimated', *Nature Communications* 12, no. 1 (2021): 1–10, p. 2.

81   United Nations Environment Program (UNEP), ed., *Assessing Global Land Use: Balancing Consumption with Sustainable Supply* (Nairobi: United Nations Environment Program, 2014), p. 25; IPBES, ed., *Global Assessment Report on Biodiversity and Ecosystem Services of the Intergovernmental Science-Policy Platform on Biodiversity and Ecosystem Services* (Bonn: IPBES, 2019).

82   The Global Living Planet Index shows the populations of mammals, birds, reptiles and fish declining by an average of 68 percent between 1970 and 2016. Up to one million species are currently threatened with extinction, about half of them because of habitat destruction, cf. Food and Agriculture Organization (FAO) and UNEP, eds., *The State of the World's Forests 2020: Forests, Biodiversity and People* (Rome: Food and Agriculture Organization, 2020), p. 12; IRP, ed., *Assessing Global Land Use: Balancing Consumption with Sustainable Supply: A Report of the Working Group on Land and Soils of the International Resource Panel*, op. cit., p. 27; IPBES, ed., *Global Assessment Report on Biodiversity and Ecosystem Services of the Intergovernmental Science-Policy Platform on Biodiversity and Ecosystem Services*, op. cit., p. 119.

83   Reckwitz, *The Society of Singularities*, op. cit.

84   Reliable sources on the total number of cars globally are few and far between, giving estimates at best: International Organization of Motor Vehicle Manufacturers (IOICA), 'World Vehicles in Use – All Vehicles', IOICA website, 2022; Andrew Chesterton, 'How Many Cars Are There in the World?', Cars Guide website, 20 September 2018.

85   Jeremy Rifkin, *Zero Marginal Cost Society: The Internet of Things, the Collaborative Commons, and the Eclipse of Capitalism* (New York: St Martin's Griffin, 2015).

86   In order to meet the global demand for electricity for all ICT devices using pedal-powered generators, the entire world population would have to 'pedal round the clock in consecutive eight-hour shifts'; Steffen Lange and Tilman Santarius, *Smarte*

grüne Welt? Digitalisierung zwischen Überwachung, Konsum und Nachhaltigkeit (Munich: Oekom, 2018), p. 27.

87 Lange and Santarius, *Smarte grüne Welt?*, op. cit.

88 Lessenich, *Neben uns die Sintflut*, op. cit.; Göran Therborn, 'The Killing Fields of Inequality', *International Journal of Health Services* 42, no. 4 (2012), pp. 579–589.

89 Cf. Stephen Emmott, *Ten Billion* (New York: Vintage, 2013).

90 Jem Bendell, *Deep Adaptation: A Map for Navigating Climate Tragedy*, IFLAS Occasional Paper 2 (2018); see also Jem Bendell and Rupert Read, eds., *Deep Adaptation: Navigating the Realities of Climate Chaos* (Cambridge and Medford: Polity, 2018); Servigne and Stevens, *How Everything Can Collapse*, op. cit.

91 Mark Pelling, *Adaptation to Climate Change: From Resilience to Transformation* (London: Routledge, 2010).

92 Bendell, *Deep Adaptation*, op. cit.

93 Ibid.

94 Ibid.

3. Modernity adé

1 Theodor W. Adorno, *Critical Models: Interventions and Catchwords*, trans. Henry W. Pickford (New York: Colombia University Press, 2005 [original German 1969]), p. 150.

2 Reinhart Koselleck and Christian Meier, 'Fortschritt', in *Geschichtliche Grundbegriffe: Historisches Lexikon zur politisch-sozialen Sprache in Deutschland*, vol. 2, ed. Otto Brunner, Werner Conze and Reinhart Koselleck, pp. 351–423 (Stuttgart: Klett-Cotta, 1997).

3 Ibid., p. 352.

4 Ibid., p. 353.

5 Sighard Neckel, 'Im Angesicht der Katastrophe', *Blätter für deutsche und internationale Politik*, February 2021, pp. 51–58.

6 Tsing, *The Mushroom at the End of the World*, op. cit., p. 21.

7 The Shell Youth Survey has been surveying the attitudes and expectations of young people in Germany at regular intervals since 1953. The ninth survey in 1981 investigated a sample of

1,077 young people aged between 15 and 24; Jugendwerk der Deutschen Shell, ed., *Jugend '81: Lebensentwürfe, Alltagskulturen, Zukunftsbilder: Studie im Auftrag des Jugendwerks der Deutschen Shell* (Opladen: Leske Budrich, 1982).

8   Jugendwerk der Deutschen Shell, ed., *Jugend '81*, op. cit., pp. 384–385.

9   Ibid., pp. 387–388, trans. MD (emphasis in original).

10   The 2002 Shell Youth Survey was the first to identify a pragmatic attitude prioritising personal life, family and career. The same phenomenon was observed in the 2006, 2010 and 2015 surveys, with a growing aspect of politicisation. The 2019 survey found that the youth were more polarised, but still 'weaving these new orientations into a pragmatic underlying pattern'. Mathias Albert, Klaus Hurrelmann and Gudrun Quenzel, *Jugend 2019: Eine Generation meldet sich zu Wort* (Weinheim and Basel: Beltz 2019), p. 323, trans. MD; cf. Hurrelmann and Albert, *Jugend 2002: Zwischen pragmatischem Idealismus und robustem Materialismus* (Frankfurt am Main: Fischer, 2004); Hurrelmann and Albert, *Jugend 2006: Eine pragmatische Generation unter Druck* (Frankfurt am Main: Fischer, 2006); Albert, Hurrelmann and Quenzel, *Jugend 2010: Eine pragmatische Generation behauptet sich* (Frankfurt am Main: Fischer, 2010); Albert, Hurrelmann and Quenzel, *Jugend 2015: Eine pragmatische Generation im Aufbruch* (Frankfurt am Main: Fischer, 2015).

11   In 2002, only 34 percent of all young people surveyed said they were interested in politics. In 1984, the figure was 55 percent, in the latest study (2019) it is 45 percent; Albert, Hurrelmann and Quenzel, *Jugend 2019*, op. cit., p. 49.

12   Ibid., p. 20.

13   Ibid.

14   Beck, *Die Erfindung des Politischen*, pp. 57ff.

15   Beck, *The Reinvention of Politics*, op. cit., pp. 32ff.

16   This is also reflected in a representative psychological survey with 1,000 participants conducted by the Rheingold-Institut in August 2021, during the Covid-19 pandemic. Like the Shell Youth Surveys, it identified a major discrepancy between expectations for the future and realities in the here and

now. While 64 percent of participants were optimistic about their personal prospects, 59 percent were pessimistic about the future of society. Here, again, there are indications that experiences of self-efficacy and agency in the private sphere can rub off onto other areas. Many respondents agreed that their actions in the personal sphere contributed to a better future – for example, demonstrating civic courage (77 percent) or providing a good example for others (89 percent). Rheingold Institut, *Psychologische Grundlagenstudie: Zum Stimmungs- und Zukunftsbild in Deutschland: Ergebnisbericht*, Erstellt für Identity Foundation – Gemeinnützige Stiftung für Philosophie (Cologne: Rheingold Institut, 2021).

17   Markus Promberger et al., 'Chancen des Resilienzbegriffes für eine soziologische Armutsforschung', in *Resilienz im Sozialen: Theoretische und empirische Analysen*, ed. Martin Endreß and Andrea Maurer, pp. 265–294 (Wiesbaden: Springer, 2015); Bröckling, *Gute Hirten führen sanft*, op. cit.

18   Suniya S. Luthar, Dante Cicchetti and Bronwyn Becker, 'The Construct of Resilience: A Critical Evaluation and Guidelines for Future Work', *Child Development* 71, no. 3 (2000), pp. 543–562.

19   Stefanie Graefe and Karina Becker, eds., *Mit Resilienz durch die Krise? Anmerkungen zu einem gefragten Konzept* (Munich: Oekom, 2021).

20   Internet platforms also promoted services promising to enhance personal well-being. The University of Pennsylvania and the Austrian Institut für Gesundheit und Entwicklung für Menschen und Organisationen (https://www.resilienzst udie.com), for example, offered personal resilience checks in connection with their research into the effects of the Covid-19 pandemic.

21   Carl Folke, 'Resilience: The Emergence of a Perspective for Social-Ecological Systems Analyses', *Global Environmental Change* 16, no. 3 (2006), pp. 253–267; Marjolein Sterk et al., 'How to Conceptualize and Operationalize Resilience in Socio-Ecological Systems?', *Current Opinion in Environmental Sustainability* 28 (2017), pp. 108–113.

22   Crawford S. Holling, 'Resilience and Stability of Ecological Systems', *Annual Review of Ecology and Systematics* 4 (1973), pp. 1–23.

23   Endreß and Maurer, eds., *Resilienz im Sozialen*, op. cit.

24   Cf. Stefan Kaufmann, 'Resilienz als Sicherheitsprogramm: Zum Janusgesicht eines Leitprogramms', in Endreß and Maurer, eds., *Resilienz im Sozialen*, op. cit., pp. 295–312; Andreas Folkers, *Das Sicherheitsdispositiv der Resilienz: Katastrophische Risiken und die Biopolitik vitaler Systeme* (Frankfurt and New York: Campus, 2018).

25   See, for example, Stefan Kaufmann's study of a framework drafted by the Homeland Security Studies and Analysis Institute, in Kaufmann, 'Resilienz als Sicherheitsprogramm', op. cit., p. 303.

26   Wolfgang Bonß, 'Karriere und sozialwissenschaftliche Potenziale des Resilienzbegriffs', in Endreß and Maurer, eds., *Resilienz im Sozialen*, op. cit., pp. 15–32.

27   The conflicts over wind farms, high-voltage transmission lines, and afforestation projects in developing countries provide a taste of the potential for discontent. For example, after COP26 the Indonesian environment minister backtracked on his country's commitment to end deforestation, on the basis that economic development came first. For the Glasgow Leaders' Declaration on Forests and Land Use see: https://ukcop26.or g/glasgow-leaders-declaration-on-forests-and-land-use/. On this aspect more generally, see Franz Walter, *Die neue Macht der Bürger: Was motiviert die Protestbewegungen? BP-Gesellschaftsstudie* (Reinbek bei Hamburg: Rowohlt, 2013).

28   David Chandler and Julian Reid, *The Neoliberal Subject: Resilience, Adaptation and Vulnerability* (Lanham: Rowman & Littlefield Publishers, 2016); Stefanie Graefe, *Resilienz im Krisenkapitalismus: Wider das Lob der Anpassungsfähigkeit* (Bielefeld: transcript, 2019); Bröckling, *Gute Hirten führen sanft*, op. cit.

29   Chandler and Reid, *The Neoliberal Subject*, op. cit.

30   Ibid., p. 78.

31   Graefe, *Resilienz im Krisenkapitalismus*, op. cit., p. 130.

32   Ibid., p. 41.

33   Ulrich Bröckling, *The Entrepreneurial Self: Fabricating a New Type of Subject* (Los Angeles et al.: Sage, 2016).

34   Graefe, *Resilienz im Krisenkapitalismus*, op. cit., p. 139.

35   Ibid., p. 151.

36   Bröckling, *Gute Hirten führen sanft*, op. cit., p. 137, trans. MD.

37   Graefe, *Resilienz im Krisenkapitalismus*, op. cit., p. 143.

38   Andreas Reckwitz, 'Lehren aus der Coronakrise: Die Politik der Resilienz hat vier Probleme', *Der Spiegel*, 5 March 2021, trans. MD.

39   Ibid.

40   Ibid.

41   Ibid.

42   Andreas Reckwitz, 'Auf dem Weg zu einer Soziologie des Verlusts', *Soziopolis*, 6 May 2021, trans. MD.

43   Ibid.

44   In response to liberal modernisation, late modernity is also witnessing a resurgence of conservatism as the modern ideology concerned with the prevention of loss; cf. Karl Mannheim, *Konservatismus: Ein Beitrag zur Soziologie des Wissens* (Frankfurt am Main: Suhrkamp, 1984).

45   Reckwitz, 'Auf dem Weg zu einer Soziologie des Verlusts', op. cit.

4. Adaptive rebellion

1   Berlin, 'Zwei Freiheitsbegriffe', op. cit.

2   Hartmut Rosa, *Resonance: A Sociology of Our Relationship to the World* (Cambridge, UK, and Medford, Mass.: Polity, 2019), epub version.

3   'Social modernity'; see Oliver Nachtwey, *Germany's Hidden Crisis: Social Decline in the Heart of Europe*, trans. Loren Balhorn and David Fernbach (London and New York: Verso, 2018). Incidentally, this is also the juncture at which the seeds of the 'artistic critique' were planted in Western societies; Luc Boltanski and Ève Chiapello, *The New Spirit of Capitalism*, trans. Gregory Elliot (London and New York: Verso, 2007).

4   John Kenneth Galbraith, *The Affluent Society* (Boston: Houghton Mifflin, 1958).

5   Ludwig Erhard was West Germany's minister of economic affairs from 1949 to 1963 and Chancellor from 1963 to 1966. Ludwig Erhard, *Wohlstand für Alle* (Düsseldorf: Econ, 1957).

6   Marshall Sahlins, *Stone Age Economics* (London: Routledge Classics, 2017 [1972]).

7   David Graeber, 'Foreword', in Marshall Sahlins, *Stone Age Economics*, op. cit., pp. ix–xviii.

8   The concept of compliance is closely associated with Max Weber's exploration of legitimate authority. The term describes the phenomenon of submission to a legitimate order; cf. Max Weber, *Economy and Society: A New Translation*, ed. and trans. Keith Tribe (Cambridge, Mass., and London: Harvard University Press, 2019 [1921]), pp. 338–447; cf. Wolfgang Fach, 'Gouvernementalité und governance: Max Webers Herrschaftssoziologie heute', in Müller and Sigmund, eds., *Max-Weber-Handbuch*, op. cit., pp. 432–434.

9   Rosa, *Resonance*, op. cit., pp. 879–892.

10   Andrew Abbott, 'The Problem of Excess', *Sociological Theory* 32, no. 1 (2014), pp.1–26.

11   Sahlins, *Stone Age Economics*, op. cit., p. 2.

12   Rosa, *Unverfügbarkeit*, op. cit.

13   Sahlins, *Stone Age Economics*, op. cit., p. 18. Here Sahlins is citing Frederick D. McCarthy and Margaret McArthur, 'The Food Quest and the Time Factor in Aboriginal Economic Life', in *Records of the Australian-American Scientific Expedition to Arnhem Land*, vol. 2: *Anthropology and Nutrition*, ed. C. P. Mountford (Melbourne: Melbourne University Press, 1960), p. 148.

14   Graeber, 'Foreword', op. cit.

15   Hartmut Rosa, 'Best Account: Outlining a Systematic Theory of Modern Society', in Reckwitz and Rosa, *Late Modernity in Crisis*, op. cit., pp. 95–157.

16   Sahlins, *Stone Age Economics*, op. cit., p. 14.

17   Ibid., p. 33.

18   Sahlins himself concedes this, but argues that his theory is applicable to most hunter-gatherer societies; cf. Sahlins, *Stone Age Economics*, op. cit., pp. 36–37.

19   For example, contrasting the life of the hunter-gatherers with J. K. Galbraith's society of limited resources and unlimited desires (which he called the 'Galbraithean way'); see Sahlins, *Stone Age Economics*, op. cit., p. 2.

20   Karl Mannheim, *Ideologie und Utopie* (Bonn: Cohen, 1930).

21   The sociological schools discussed above focus either on order and stability or on power and liberty. In the former, adaptation occurs more or less automatically as the fundamental cultural consensus of the society (*viz.*, Parsons). Sociologies centring on freedom tend to regard adaptation as the antithesis of a generative and transformative praxis. Instead, it is a synonym for the stabilisation of an inherently defective order.

22   Robert K. Merton, 'Social Structure and Anomie', *American Sociological Review* 3, no. 5 (1938), pp. 672–682.

23   Ibid., p. 678.

24   Ibid.

25   Ibid., p. 677.

26   Robert K. Merton, 'Social Structure and Anomie', in *On Social Structure and Science*, pp. 133–152 (Chicago: University of Chicago Press, 1996), here p. 151.

27   Karl Mannheim, 'Das Problem der Generationen', in *Wissenssoziologie: Auswahl aus dem Werk*, ed. Kurt H. Wolff, pp. 509–565 (Berlin and Neuwied: Luchterhand, 1964 [1928]).

28   Heinz Bude, *Deutsche Karrieren: Lebenskonstruktionen sozialer Aufsteiger aus der Flakhelfer-Generation* (Frankfurt am Main: Suhrkamp, 1987), p. 425, trans. MD.

29   Dieter Rucht, *Modernisierung und neue soziale Bewegungen: Deutschland, Frankreich und USA im Vergleich* (Frankfurt am Main and New York: Campus, 1994).

30   Cf. Boltanski and Chiapello, *The New Spirit of Capitalism*, op. cit.

31   While Dieter Rucht doubts whether Fridays for Future speaks for an entire generation, Klaus Hurrelmann and Erik Albrecht see climate issues as just the start of the politicisation of 'Generation Greta'; cf. Dieter Rucht, 'Jugend auf der Straße: Fridays

for Future und die Generationenfrage', *WZB-Mitteilungen*, no. 165 (2019), pp. 6–9; Klaus Hurrelmann and Erik Albrecht, *Generation Greta: Was sie denkt, wie sie fühlt und warum das Klima erst der Anfang ist* (Weinheim and Basel: Beltz, 2020).

32   Mattias Wahlström et al., eds., *Protest for a Future: Composition, Mobilization and Motives of the Participants in Fridays for Future Climate Protests on 15 March 2019 in 13 European Cities* (N.p.: Protest Institute, 2019); Moritz Sommer et al., 'Fridays for Future: Profil, Entstehung und Perspektiven der Protestbewegung in Deutschland', *Internationale Politik* 74, no. 4 (2019), pp. 121–125.

33   Sommer et al., 'Fridays for Future', op. cit., p. 10. Note that the study excluded subjects younger than fourteen years of age.

34   Sommer et al., 'Fridays for Future', op. cit., p. 13.

35   Wahlström et al., eds., *Protest for a Future*, op. cit., p. 9.

36   Hurrelmann and Albrecht, *Generation Greta*, op. cit., p. 188.

37   Laura Backes et al., 'Kinder der Apokalypse', *Der Spiegel*, 31 May 2019.

38   It is no coincidence that the prominent German climate activists Luisa Neubauer and Alexander Repenning subtitle their book 'A History of Our Future'. *Beginning to End the Climate Crisis* is an appeal to what they call the 'possibilists': forward-thinking individuals who recognise possibilities and seek to realise them. Rather than looking for a secure future, they are thinking in the conjunctive: 'the future is no longer a promise'. Luisa-Marie Neubauer and Alexander Repenning, *Beginning to End the Climate Crisis: A History of Our Future* (Waltham, Mass.: Brandeis University Press, 2023 [2019]), p. 13).

39   Adorno, *Critical Models: Interventions and Catchwords*, op. cit., p. 29.

40   In 2021, the Fridays for Future movement laid out the following concrete demands for the first one hundred days of the new German government: a CO_2 budget in line with the 1.5°C target, no new natural gas infrastructure and a complete end to its use by 2035; an end to subsidies for fossil fuels and no expansion of lignite mining; a sevenfold increase in solar and wind power and removal of any political obstacles to their expansion; no manufacture of internal combustion engines from 2025 and

an immediate stop to all major roadbuilding projects; 14 billion euros annually for international climate financing; all trade
agreements to conform with human rights and climate targets.
The list is available online at https://fridaysforfuture.de/forder
ungen/100-tage/ (as of June 2022).

41   Neubauer and Repenning, *Beginning to End the Climate Crisis*, op.
cit., p. 53.

42   Ernst Friedrich Schumacher, *Small Is Beautiful: A Study of Economics as If People Mattered* (London: Blond & Briggs, 1973).

43   Sahlins, *Stone Age Economics*, op. cit., p. 2.

44   Ingolfur Blühdorn, 'Haben wir es gewollt? Vorüberlegungen',
in Blühdorn et al., *Nachhaltige Nicht-Nachhaltigkeit*, op. cit., pp.
13–28, here p. 17.

45   Blühdorn, 'Die Gesellschaft der Nicht-Nachhaltigkeit', op. cit.,
p. 113, trans. MD.

46   Strategic in the sense that the cited scientific findings back up
their own positions and neutralise those of their adversaries.

47   Ingolfur Blühdorn, 'Demokratie der Nicht-Nachhaltigkeit:
Begehung eines umweltsoziologischen Minenfeldes', in
Blühdorn et al., *Nachhaltige Nicht-Nachhaltigkeit*, op. cit., pp.
303–344, here p. 323.

48   Beck, *The Reinvention of Politics*, op. cit., p. 107–108.

49   Hartmut Rosa's concept of the 'medio-passive' builds on philo-
sophical debates seeking a middle way between perpetrator
and victim, dependency and autonomy, and active and passive.
Such a medio-passive relationship to the world, he argues, can
pave the way for a comprehensive transformation by doing
away with the outdated sovereignty paradigm of modernity.
Cf. Hartmut Rosa, „Spirituelle Abhängigkeitserklärung": Die
Idee des Mediopassiv als Ausgangspunkt einer radikalen
Transformation', in *Große Transformation? Zur Zukunft moderner
Gesellschaften*, special issue of *Berliner Journal für Soziologie*, ed.
Klaus Dörre et al., pp. 35–56 (Wiesbaden: Springer, 2019). For
a discussion in English, see Hartmut Rosa, 'Resonance as a
Medio-Passive, Emancipatory and Transformative Power: A
Reply to My Critics', *Journal of Chinese Sociology* 10, art. no. 16
(2023).

5. Criticality and critique: The avant-gardes of adaptation

1   Tsing, *The Mushroom at the End of the World*, op. cit., p. 28.

2   Ève Chiapello, 'Capitalism and Its Criticism', in *New Spirits of Capitalism*, ed. Glenn Morgan and Paul du Gay, pp. 60–82 (Oxford: Oxford University Press, 2013).

3   Mannheim, *Ideologie und Utopie*, op. cit.

4   Chiapello, 'Capitalism and Its Criticism', op. cit., p. 25.

5   Luc Boltanski, *Soziologie und Sozialkritik* (Berlin: Suhrkamp, 2010); Boltanski and Chiapello, *The New Spirit of Capitalism*, op. cit.

6   Streeck, *Gekaufte Zeit*, op. cit.

7   Boltanski and Chiapello, *The New Spirit of Capitalism*, op. cit.

8   Chiapello, 'Capitalism and Its Criticism', op. cit., pp. 60–82.

9   Boltanski and Chiapello, *The New Spirit of Capitalism*, op. cit.

10   The artistic critique has itself been criticised for accepting an erosion of civil rights and social security, and, as such, doing less to promote democracy than the preceding wave of social protests.

11   Chiapello, 'Capitalism and Its Criticism', op. cit., p. 16.

12   At the beginning of the pandemic it was believed that only certain high-risk groups would be severely affected.

13   For a detailed analysis of shifting views on working from home during the pandemic, see Infas and Institut für Wirtschaftsforschung, *Homeoffice im Verlauf der Corona-Pandemie*, Themenreport Corona Plattform, July 2021.

14   Steffen Mau, *Sortiermaschinen: Die Neuerfindung der Grenze im 21. Jahrhundert* (Munich: C. H. Beck, 2021).

15   Neckel, *Im Angesicht der Katastrophe*, op. cit.

16   Andreas Malm, *Corona, Climate, Chronic Emergency: War Communism in the Twenty-First Century* (London and New York: Verso, 2020).

17   This applies whatever the true origins of the Covid-19 virus, about which doubts remain. The widely accepted theory that the virus passed from animals to humans would place it in the context of increased likelihood of zoonoses when settlement expansion brings people into closer contact with wild animals;

cf. Malm, *Corona, Climate, Chronic Emergency*, op. cit. If the virus ultimately transpires to have originated in a laboratory, the pandemic will have been even more obviously anthropogenic.

18   Frank Adloff and Sighard Neckel, 'Wettlauf gegen die Zeit: Agenda für eine neue Regierung im Klimajahrzehnt', *Blätter für deutsche und internationale Politik*, October 2021, pp. 55–62.

19   Suddenly, the telecommunications engineer found herself responsible for a service deemed of vital importance for society. Hospitals and supermarkets were recognised as essential services. At least for a time, there was a broadly shared realisation that the superficial temptations of the modern economy could not exist without the underlying collective practices of reproduction. It is the key workers in this 'foundational economy' who ensure the technical and social reproduction of society; cf. The Foundational Economy Collective, *Foundational Economy: The Infrastructure of Everyday Life* (Manchester, UK: Manchester University Press, 2018).

20   Eva Barlösius, *Infrastrukturen als soziale Ordnungsdienste: Ein Beitrag zur Gesellschaftsdiagnose* (Frankfurt am Main and New York: Campus, 2019).

21   In this research project, students conducted and evaluated seventy-nine narrative interviews with essential workers from the fields of health, education, childcare, public order and material infrastructure. The interviews were conducted between spring 2020 and spring 2022. The goal was to explore the experiences of essential workers and their thoughts about society. The research covered four fields: healthcare, education/childcare, public order and material infrastructure. The interviews focussed on the subjects' views on the response to the pandemic and their associated ideas about society. The analysis employed the documentary method developed by Ralf Bohnsack on the basis of Mannheim's sociology of knowledge to elucidate subjective meaning and implicit forms of knowledge. I am grateful to the participants in my master seminar on criticality and criticism, who conducted the fieldwork and analysis. The interviews were conducted in German; the extracts have been translated into English. Cf. Ralf Bohn-

sack, Iris Nentwig-Gesemann and Arnd-Michael Nohl, *Die dokumentarische Methode und ihre Forschungspraxis*, Grundlagen qualitativer Sozialforschung (Wiesbaden: Springer, 2013).

22　Annekatrin Schrenker, Claire Samtleben and Markus Schrenker, 'Applaus ist nicht genug: Gesellschaftliche Anerkennung systemrelevanter Berufe', *Aus Politik und Zeitgeschichte* 71 (2021), pp. 13–15, trans. MD.

23　Ibid.

24　Roughly 70 percent of essential workers in Germany earn less than the average wage. In comparison to the labour market as a whole, they are more likely to be on temporary contracts and more likely to be worried about their own economic situation – even though they are actually more likely to be covered by collective pay agreements (because of the prominent role of the public sector in these spheres); cf. Schrenker, Samtleben and Schrenker, 'Applaus ist nicht genug', op. cit., p. 14.

25　Nicole Mayer-Ahuja and Oliver Nachtwey, *Verkannte Leistungsträger:innen: Berichte aus der Klassengesellschaft* (Berlin: Suhrkamp, 2021).

26　Roughly 70 percent of police employees in Germany are male, cf. Statistisches Bundesamt, 'Pressemitteilung Nr. 57', 18 September 2020, https://www.destatis.de/DE/Presse/Pressemitteilungen/2020/09/PD20_N057_742.html.

27　Original German: 'Leben in der Lage'; more literally 'living in the situation'.

28　Reckwitz, *The Society of Singularities*, op. cit.

29　On the distinction between input and output legitimacy, see Fritz W. Scharpf, *Regieren in Europa: Effektiv und Demokratisch?* (Frankfurt am Main and New York: Campus, 1999).

6. Protective technocracy

1　Joseph Schumpeter, *Capitalism, Socialism and Democracy* (London and New York: Routledge, 1994 [1943]), p. 302.

2　Sophie Haring calls this 'the rule of necessity'; cf. Sophie Haring, 'Herrschaft der Experten oder Herrschaft des Sachzwangs? Technokratie als politikwissenschaftliches „Problem-Ensemble", *Zeitschrift für Politik* 57, no. 3 (2010), pp. 243–264.

3   Blühdorn, *Simulative Demokratie*, op. cit.

4   From Plato's philosopher king and Aristotle's 'bad forms' of constitution to Rousseau's belief that democracy was suitable only for small communities and Kant's outright aversion; cf. Blühdorn, *Simulative Demokratie*, op. cit., pp. 25ff.

5   Max Weber, *Economy and Society: A New Translation*, ed. and trans. Keith Tribe (Cambridge, Mass., and London, Harvard University Press: 2019 [1921]), p. 408.

6   Blühdorn, *Simulative Demokratie*, op. cit., pp. 25ff., trans. MD.

7   Schumpeter, *Capitalism, Socialism and Democracy*, op. cit., pp. 289–295.

8   Ibid., p. 291.

9   Ibid., pp. 291–293.

10 Blühdorn, *Simulative Demokratie*, op. cit., p. 40.

11 Jürgen Habermas, *Theorie des kommunikativen Handelns*, vol. 2: *Zur Kritik der funktionalistischen Vernunft* (Frankfurt am Main: Suhrkamp, 1981).

12 For a detailed description, see the Civilopedia website, 'Synthetic technocracy', https://www.civilopedia.net/gathering-storm/governments/government_synthetic_technocracy.

13 Ibid.

14 The economic (or socialist) calculation debate; cf. Ludwig von Mises, *Economic Calculation in the Socialist Commonwealth* (Auburn: Ludwig von Mises Institute, Auburn University, 1990 [1920]).

15 Evgeny Morozov, 'Digital Socialism? The Calculation Debate in the Age of Big Data', *New Left Review*, no. 116/117 (2019), pp. 33–67.

16 Nick Dyer-Witheford, 'Red plenty platforms', *Culture Machine* 14 (2013), pp. 1–27.

17 Daniel Saros, *Information Technology and Socialist Construction: The End of Capital and the Transition to Socialism* (London: Routledge, 2014); Morozov, 'Digital Socialism?' op. cit.; Jochum and Schaupp, 'Die Steuerungswende', op. cit.; Jasper Bernes, 'Planning and Anarchy', *South Atlantic Quarterly* 119, no. 1 (2020), pp. 53–73.

18   The Cybersyn project was launched by Salvador Allende's socialist government in Chile in the early 1970s. Its purpose was to coordinate the economy in real time using computerisation, cutting out market mechanisms. The heart of the system was a network of telex machines sending factory data to a central operations room in the capital. The plan was also for consumers to communicate their needs directly to the central computer via TV devices in private households. Cybersyn was never fully completed and was dismantled following Augusto Pinochet's military coup in 1973. The subsequent period saw the introduction of extreme free-market policies in Chile.

19   Bernes, 'Planning and Anarchy', op. cit.

20   Morozov, 'Digital Socialism?' op. cit.; Jochum and Schaupp, 'Die Steuerungswende', op. cit.

21   Leigh Phillips and Michal Rozworski, *The People's Republic of Walmart: How the World's Biggest Corporations Are Laying the Foundation for Socialism* (London and New York: Verso, 2019).

22   Schumpeter, *Capitalism, Socialism and Democracy*, op. cit.

23   James E. Lovelock with Bryan Appleyard, *Novacene: The Coming Age of Hyperintelligence* (Cambridge, Mass., and London: MIT Press, 2020). Lovelock is best known as the co-author of the Gaia hypothesis, according to which the earth and its biosphere form a single self-stabilising system.

24   Beck, *The Reinvention of Politics*, op. cit.

25   Stephan Lessenich, 'Die Dialektik der Demokratie: Grenzziehungen und Grenzüberschreitungen im Wohlfahrtskapitalismus', in *Was stimmt nicht mit der Demokratie?*, ed. Ketterer and Becker, op. cit., pp. 121–138.

26   Reckwitz, *The End of Illusions*, op. cit.

27   Streeck, *Zwischen Globalismus und Demokratie*, op. cit.

28   Malm, *Corona, Climate, Chronic Emergency*, op. cit.

29   Benjamin Bratton, *Revenge of the Real: Post-Pandemic Politics* (London and Oxford: Verso, 2021).

30   Ibid., pp. 33–45.

31   Ibid., p. 43.

32   Ibid., p. 145.

33   Ibid., p. 156.

34   Max Weber, 'Science as a Vocation' (1917/19) and 'Politics as a Vocation' (1919), in *Max Weber's Complete Writings on Academic and Political Vocations*, ed. and intro. by John Dreijmanis, trans. Gordon C. Wells (N.p.; Algora, 2008).

35   Max Weber, 'Science as a Vocation', op. cit., p. 35.

36   Max Weber, 'Politics as a Vocation', op. cit., p. 173.

37   Ibid., p. 207.

38   Max Weber, *Economy and Society: A New Translation*, ed. and trans. Keith Tribe (Cambridge, Mass., and London, Harvard University Press: 2019 [1921]), p. 134.

39   Thorstein Veblen, *The Engineers and the Price System* (Kitchener, Canada: Batoche Books, 2001 [1921]), p. 46. Cf. Dieter Senghaas, 'The Technocrats: Rückblick auf die Technokratiebewegung in den USA', in *Texte zur Technokratiediskussion*, ed. Claus Koch and Dieter Senghaas, pp. 282–295 (Frankfurt am Main: Europäische Verlagsanstalt, 1970), p. 285.

40   Thorstein Veblen, *The Engineers and the Price System*, op. cit.

41   Senghaas, 'The Technocrats', op. cit., p. 286.

42   These included the Technical Alliance, the Continental Comittee on Technocracy, and Technocracy, Inc.

43   Cf. Jacques Ellul, *The Technological Society* (London: Cape, 1965); Jean Meynaud, *Technocracy* (London: Faber, 1968); for a detailed discussion of the development of technocratic ideas, see Vincent August, *Technologisches Regieren: Der Aufstieg des Netzwerk-Denkens in der Krise der Moderne: Foucault, Luhmann und die Kybernetik* (Bielefeld: transcript, 2021).

44   Helmut Schelsky, *Der Mensch in der wissenschaftlichen Zivilisation* (Cologne and Opladen: Westdeutscher Verlag, 1961).

45   Ibid., p. 25, trans. MD.

46   Ibid., p. 31, trans. MD.

47   Offe was thinking of developments such as the destruction of traditional rural ways of life through technocratic agricultural policies. In a planetary technocracy of the kind sketched out by Bratton, one could imagine legitimacy issues arising from the need to reduce material consumption; cf. Claus Offe, 'Das politische Dilemma der Technokratie', in *Texte zur*

Technokratiediskussion, ed. Koch and Senghaas, op. cit., pp. 156–171.

48   Ibid., p. 163, trans. MD.

49   Ibid., p. 166.

GPSR Authorized Representative: Easy Access System Europe, Mustamäe tee
50, 10621 Tallinn, Estonia, gpsr.requests@easproject.com